POP HITS FOR KIDS

ISBN 978-1-5400-3120-4

Visit Hal Leonard Online at
www.halleonard.com

Contact Us:
Hal Leonard
7777 West Bluemound Road
Milwaukee, WI 53213
Email: info@halleonard.com

In Europe contact:
Hal Leonard Europe Limited
Distribution Centre, Newmarket Road
Bury St Edmunds, Suffolk, IP33 3YB
Email: info@halleonardeurope.com

In Australia contact:
Hal Leonard Australia Pty. Ltd.
4 Lentara Court
Cheltenham, Victoria, 3192 Australia
Email: info@halleonard.com.au

ANYWHERE

Words and Music by RITA ORA,
NICHOLAS GALE, NOLAN LAMBROZZA,
BRIAN LEE, ALEXANDRA TAMPOSI,
ANDREW WOTMAN and ALESSANDRO LINDBLAD

Moderately

Time flies by when the night is young,
Truth comes out when you're back-ing out,

day-light shines on an un-dis-closed lo-ca-tion, _____ lo-
look-ing for con-nec-tion in a crowd of emp-ty fac-es, _____ emp-ty

ca-tion. _____
fac-es. _____ Your

Blood-shot eyes look-ing for the sun,
se-crets are the on-ly thing I'm crav-ing now, the

par-a-dise de-liv-ered and we call it a va-ca-tion, _____ va-
good _____ and the bad _____ let me in 'cause I can take it, _____ I can

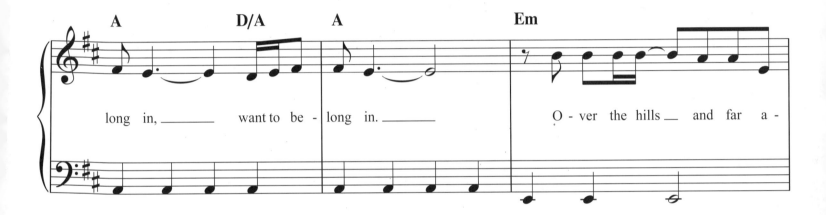

4

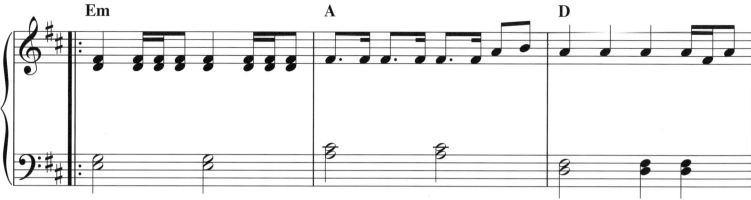

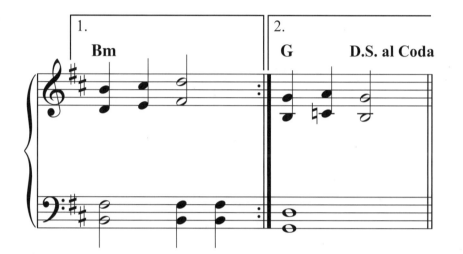

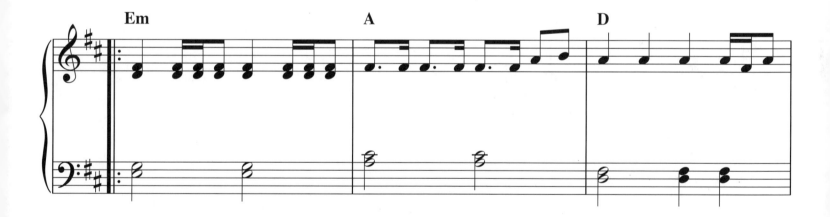

Take me an - y - where, _ oh,

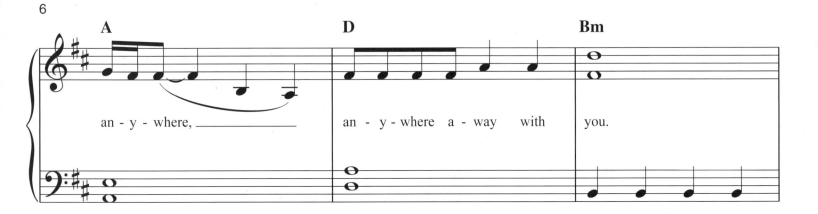

an - y - where, _____ an - y - where a - way with you.

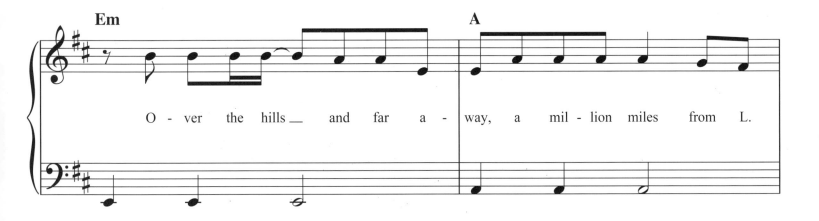

O - ver the hills __ and far a - way, a mil - lion miles from L.

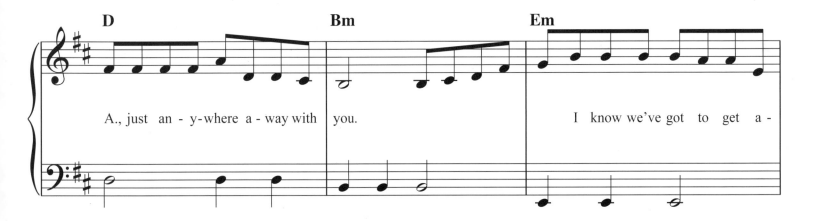

A., just an - y-where a - way with you. I know we've got to get a -

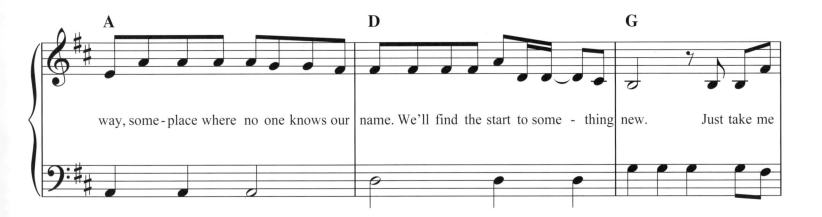

way, some - place where no one knows our name. We'll find the start to some - thing new. Just take me

an - y - where, _____ take me an - y - where, _____ an - y - where a - way with you. _____

_____ Just take me an - y - where, _____ take me an - y - where, _____

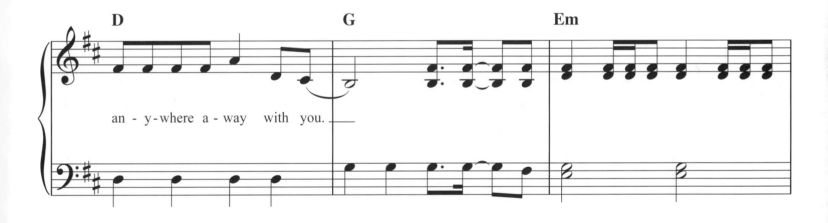

an - y - where a - way with you. _____

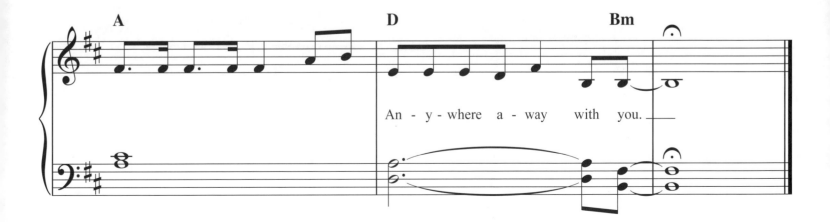

An - y - where a - way with you. _____

EVERMORE
from BEAUTY AND THE BEAST

Music by ALAN MENKEN
Lyrics by TIM RICE

Moderately slow, with freedom

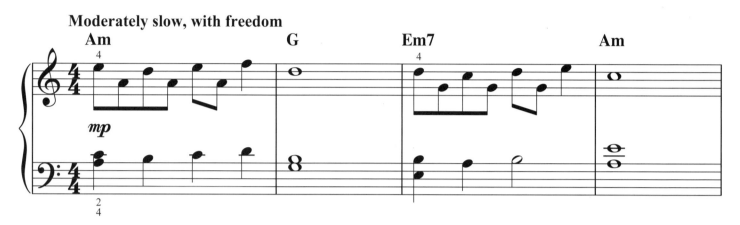

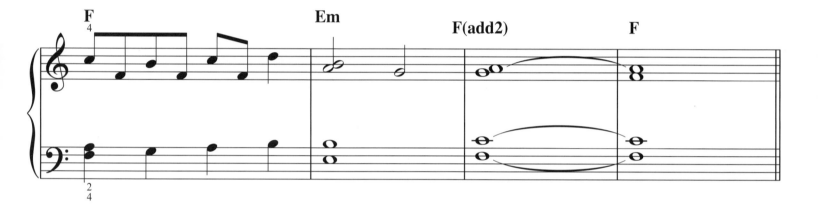

I was the one __ who had it all;
I'll nev-er shake __ a-way the pain.

I was the mas - ter of my
I close my eyes, __ but she's still

fate.
there.

I nev-er need-ed an - y - bod-y in my life;
I let her steal in - to my mel - an - chol - y heart;

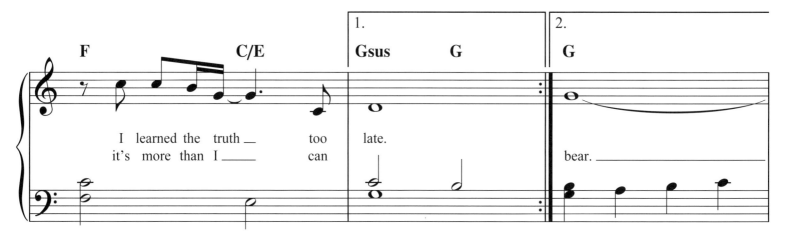

1. Gsus G   **2.** G

I learned the truth __ too late.

it's more than I ____ can   bear. _____

____ Now I know she'll nev - er leave me, e - ven as she runs a-

way. She will still tor - ment __ me, calm me, hurt __ me, move me, come what

may.   Wast - ing in ____ my lone - ly tow - er,

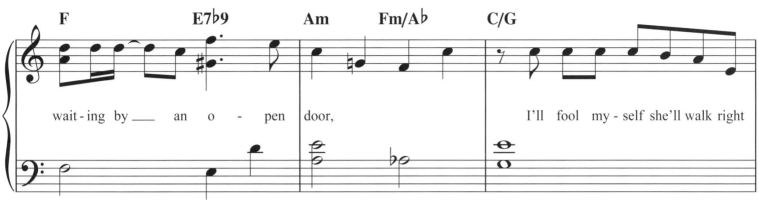

waiting by ___ an o - pen door, I'll fool my - self she'll walk right

in, and be with me for - ev - er - more.

I rage a - gainst ___ the trials of love.

I curse the fad - ing of the light. Though she's al - read - y flown so

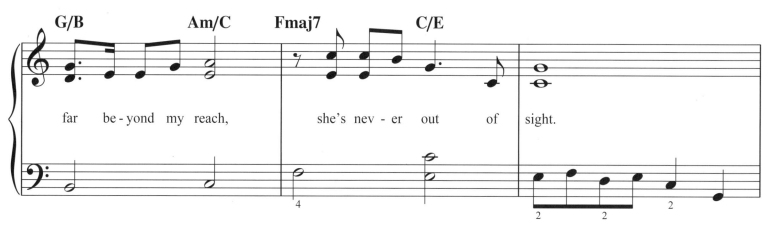

far be-yond my reach, she's nev-er out of sight.

Now I know she'll nev-er leave me, e-ven as she fades from

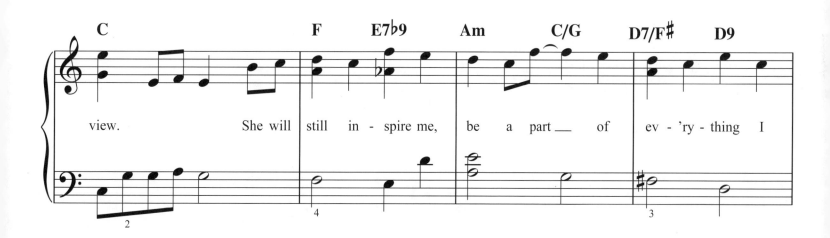

view. She will still in-spire me, be a part ___ of ev-'ry-thing I

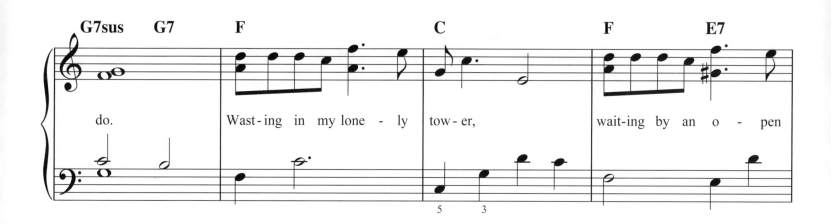

do. Wast-ing in my lone-ly tow-er, wait-ing by an o-pen

door,   I'll fool my-self she'll walk right   in,

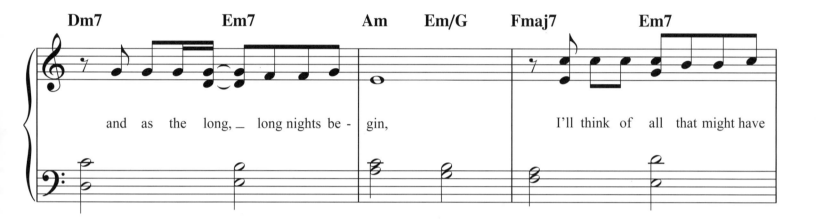

and as the long, __ long nights be - gin,   I'll think of   all   that might have

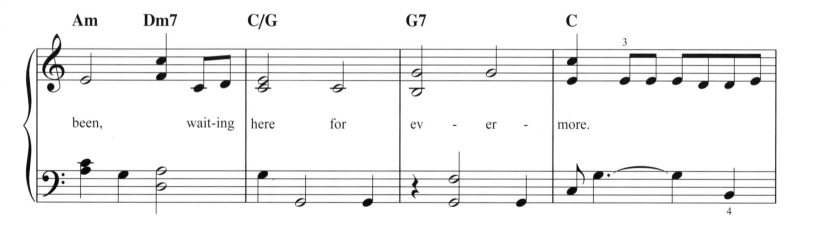

been,   wait-ing here   for   ev -   er -   more.

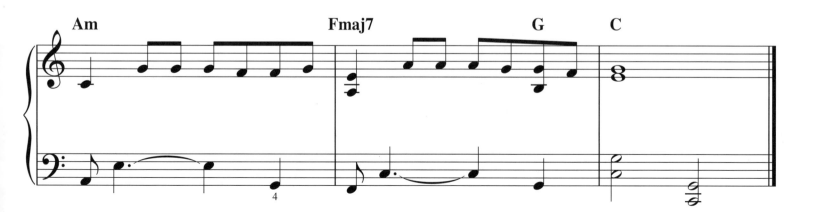

CITY OF STARS
from LA LA LAND

Music by JUSTIN HURWITZ
Lyrics by BENJ PASEK & JUSTIN PAUL

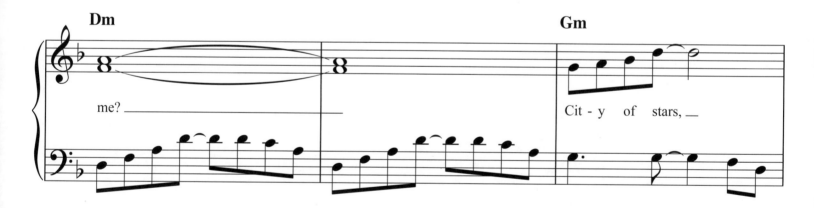

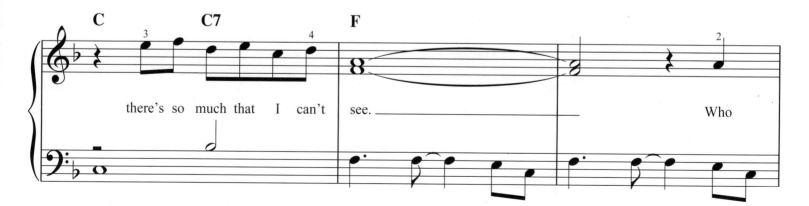

knows? I felt it from the first em - brace I shared with

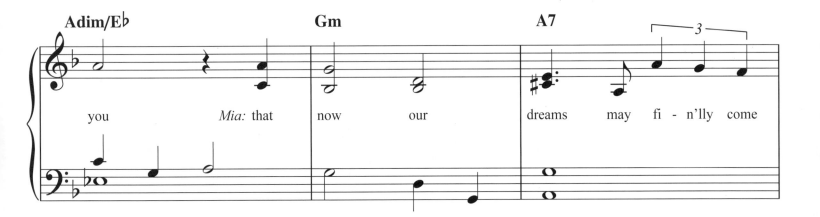

you *Mia:* that now our dreams may fi - n'lly come

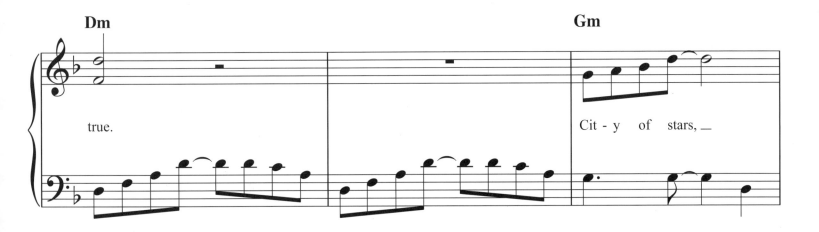

true. Cit - y of stars, —

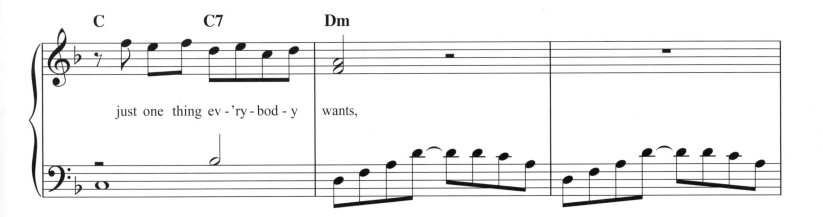

just one thing ev - 'ry - bod - y wants,

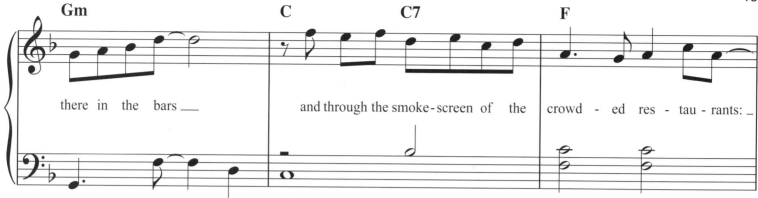

there in the bars ___ and through the smoke-screen of the crowd - ed res - tau - rants: _

___ it's love. Yes, all we're look - ing for is

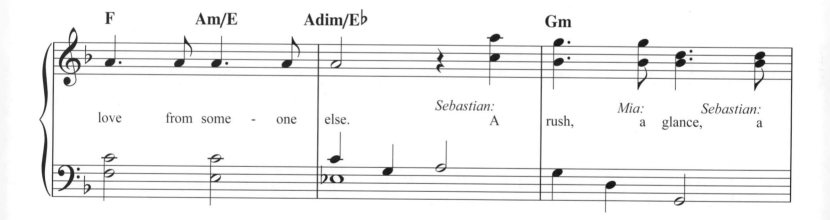

love from some - one else. *Sebastian:* A rush, *Mia:* a glance, *Sebastian:* a

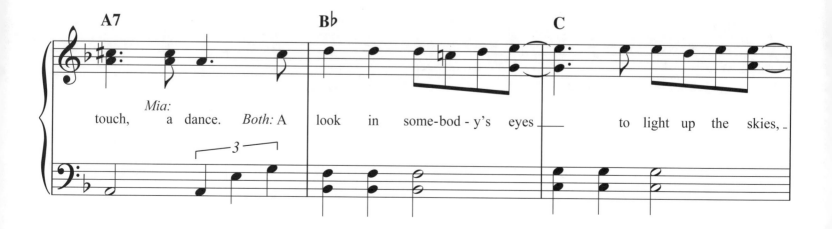

touch, *Mia:* a dance. *Both:* A look in some-bod - y's eyes ___ to light up the skies, _

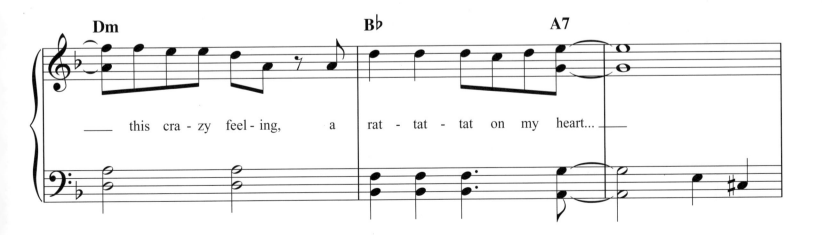

Freely   **Dm**

Sebastian: Think I want it to   stay. _____

Gm   **C7**   **F**

Cit - y of stars, __   are you shin - ing just for   me? _____

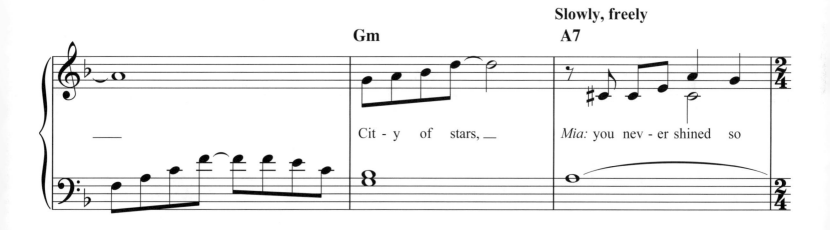

                                   Gm   **Slowly, freely**
                                               A7

___   Cit - y of stars, __   *Mia:* you nev - er shined   so

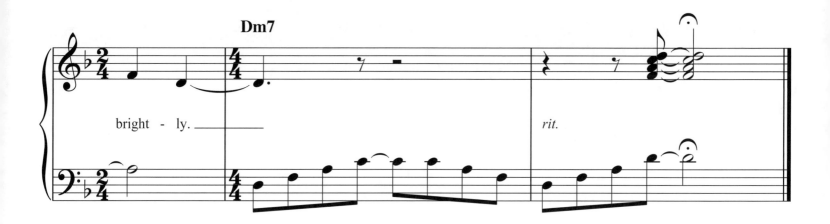

                   Dm7

bright - ly. _____   *rit.*

FEEL IT STILL

Words and Music by JOHN GOURLEY, ZACH CAROTHERS,
JASON SECHRIST, ERIC HOWK, KYLE O'QUIN,
BRIAN HOLLAND, FREDDIE GORMAN, GEORGIA DOBBINS,
ROBERT BATEMAN, WILLIAM GARRETT, JOHN HILL
and ASA TACCONE

Fast Rock

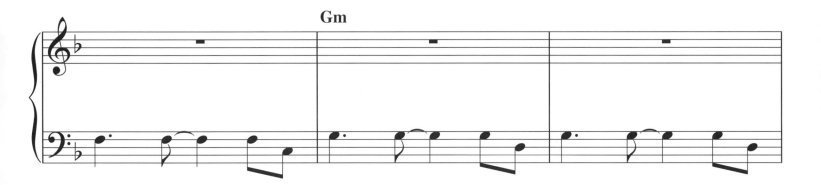

Can't keep my hands to my-self.

Think I'll dust 'em off, put 'em back up on the shelf,

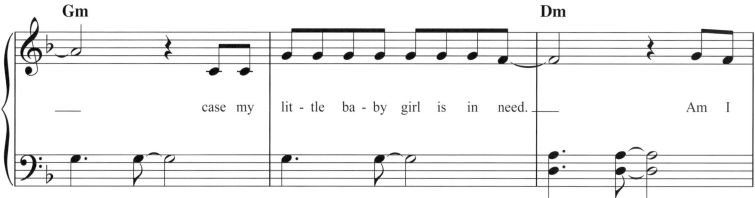

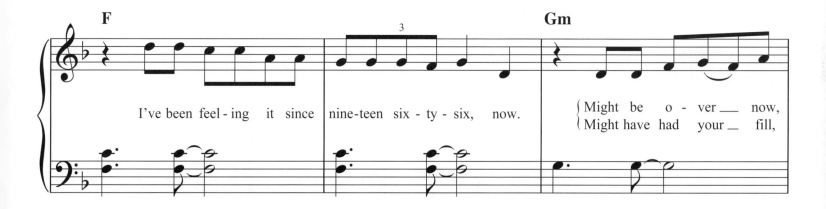

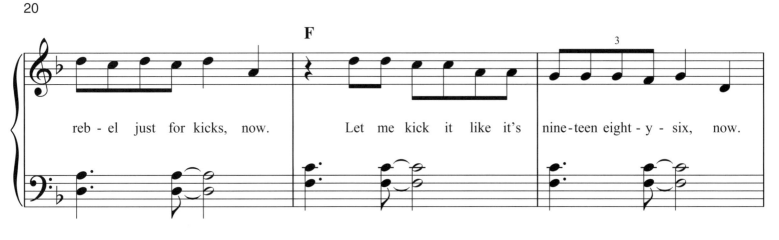

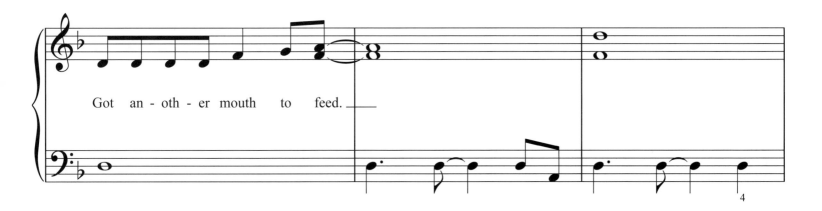

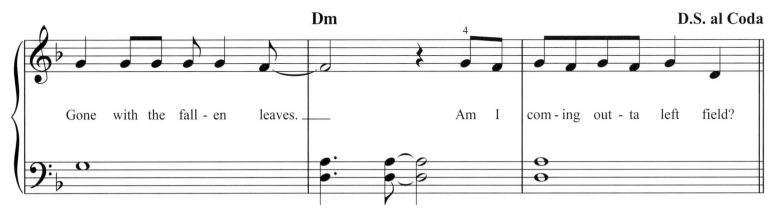
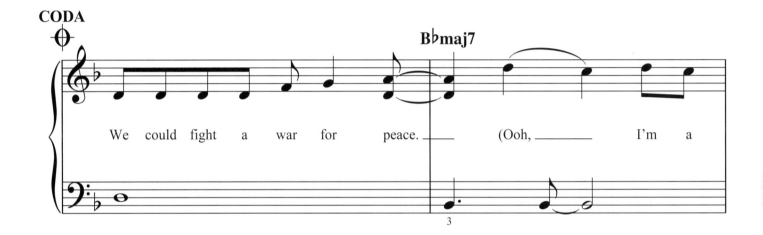
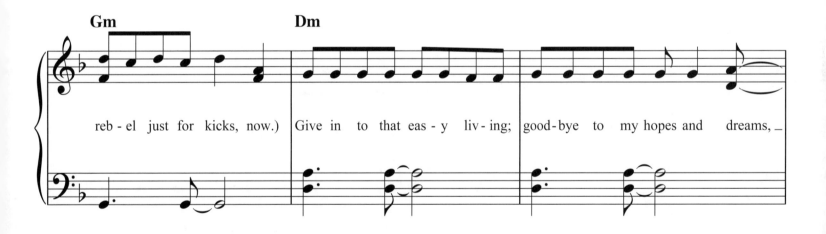
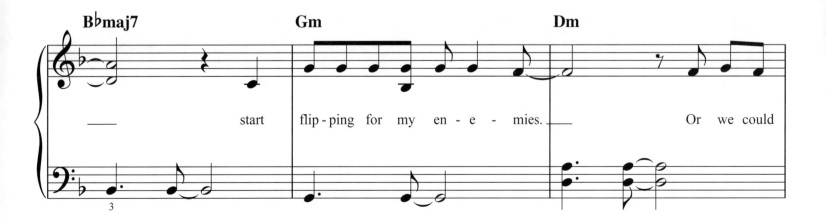

wait un - til the walls come down. ___ (Ooh, ___ I'm a reb - el just for kicks, now.) It's

time to give a lit - tle to the kids in the mid - dle, but, oh, ___ un - til ___ it falls, ___

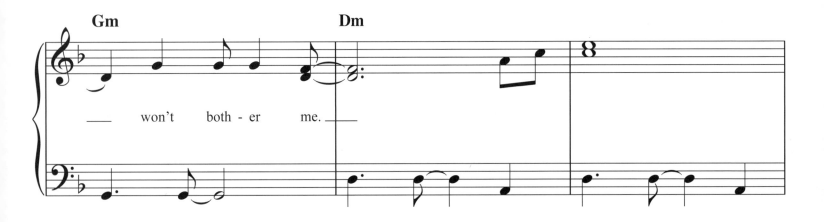

___ won't both - er me. ___

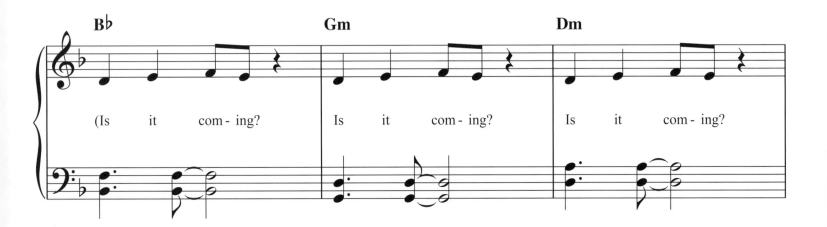

(Is it com - ing? Is it com - ing? Is it com - ing?

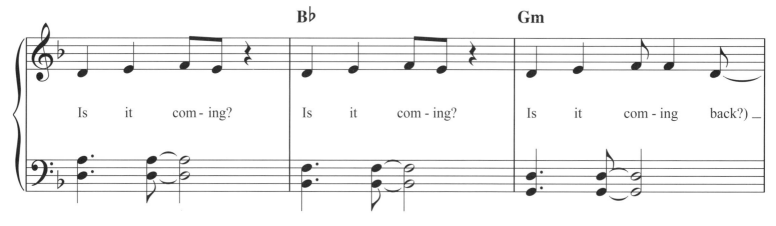

Is it com - ing? Is it com - ing? Is it com - ing back?) __

Ooh, ____ I'm a

reb - el just for kicks. Yeah, your love is an a - byss for my heart to e - clipse, now.

Might be o - ver __ now, but I feel it still.

Ooh, _____ I'm a reb - el just for kicks, now.

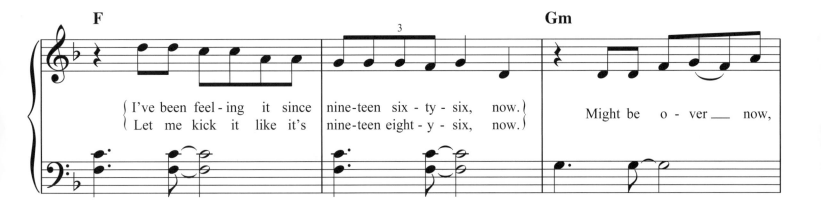

F

I've been feel - ing it since nine-teen six - ty - six, now.
Let me kick it like it's nine-teen eight - y - six, now.

Gm

Might be o - ver _____ now,

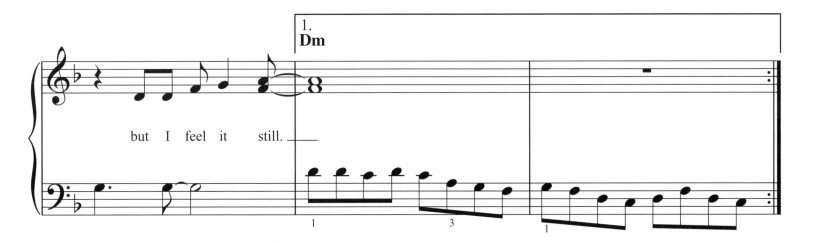

1.
Dm

but I feel it still. _____

2.
Dm

_____ Might have had your fill, but you feel it still. _____

FIGHT SONG

Words and Music by RACHEL PLATTEN
and DAVE BASSETT

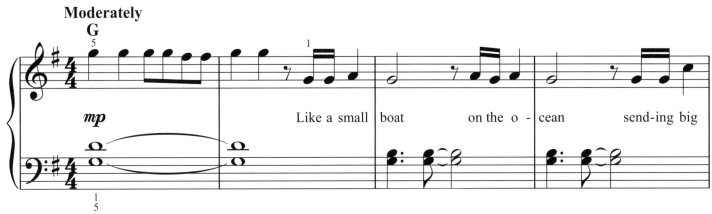

Like a small boat on the o - cean send-ing big

waves in - to mo - tion. Like how a sin - gle word can make a heart o -

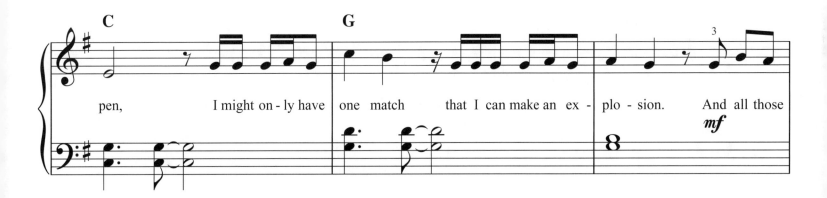

pen, I might on - ly have one match that I can make an ex - plo - sion. And all those

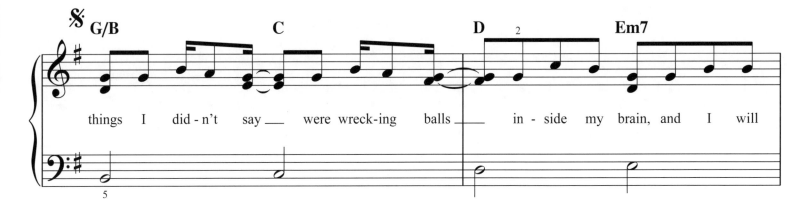

things I did - n't say ___ were wreck - ing balls ___ in - side my brain, and I will

scream 'em a-loud to-night. Can you hear my voice this time? This is my fight song, take-back-my-

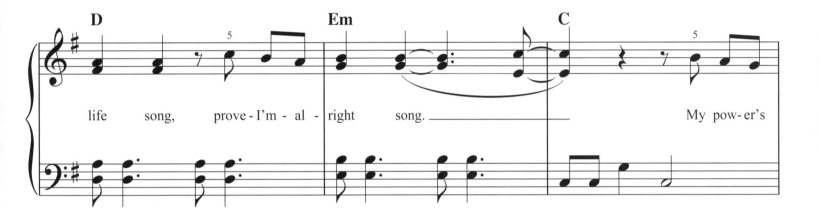

life song, prove-I'm-al-right song. _____ My pow-er's

turned on. Start-ing right now, I'll be strong. I'll play my fight song. And I

To Coda ⊕

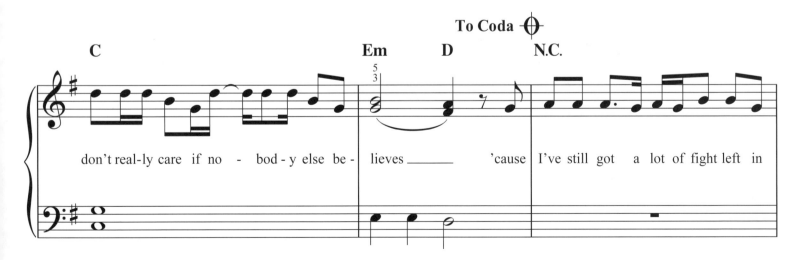

don't real-ly care if no - bod-y else be - lieves _____ 'cause I've still got a lot of fight left in

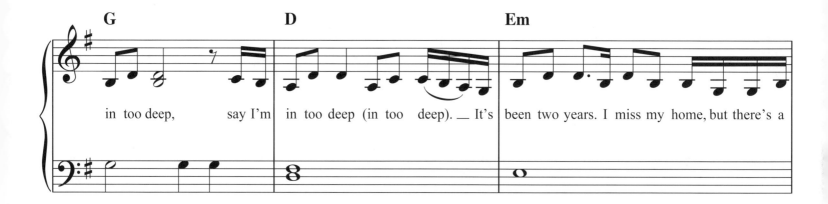

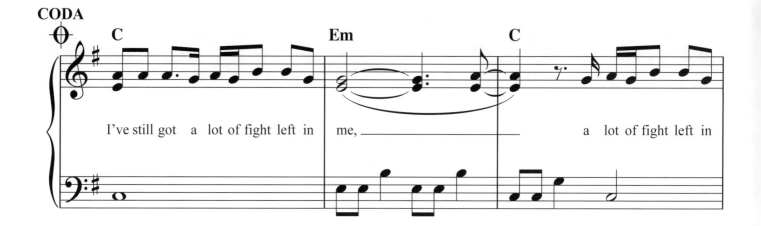

me. _____

Like a small boat on the o -

cean send-ing big waves _____ in-to mo - tion. _____ Like how a sin-gle

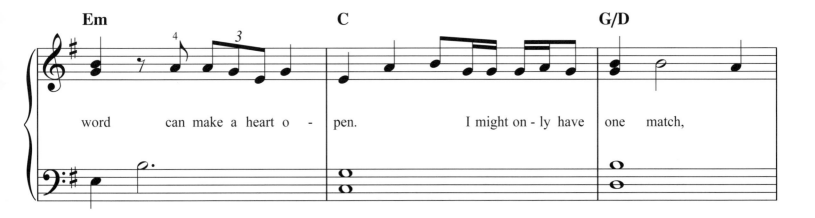

word can make a heart o - pen. I might on - ly have one match,

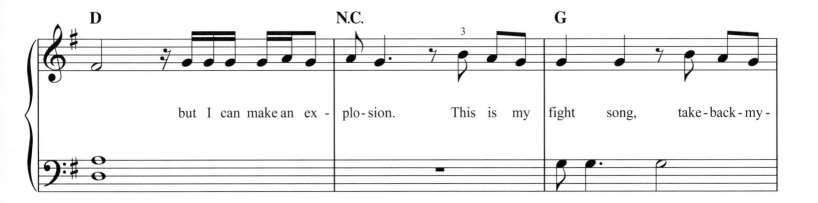

but I can make an ex - plo-sion. This is my fight song, take-back-my-

life song, prove-I'm - al - right song._____ My pow-er's

turned on. Start-ing right now, I'll be strong. I'll play my fight song. And I

don't real-ly care if no - bod - y else be - lieves_____ 'cause I've still got a lot of fight left in

me._____ No, I've still got a lot of fight left in me.

GREATEST LOVE STORY

Words and Music by
BRANDON LANCASTER

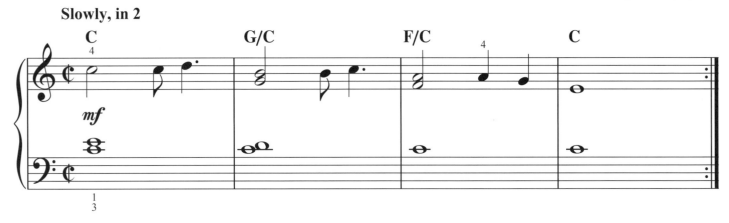

They said I was noth - in'
you went off to col - lege and

but a trou - ble - mak - er and   nev - er up to no good.
I   got a job.   I was   work - in' that nine to five.

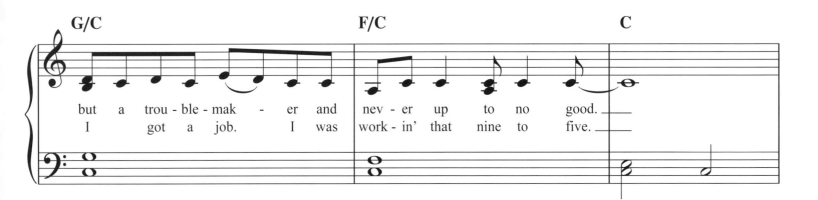

You were the per - fect all - A - mer - i - can girl, would - n't
Dream - in' of the days   when   you were in my arms, I had

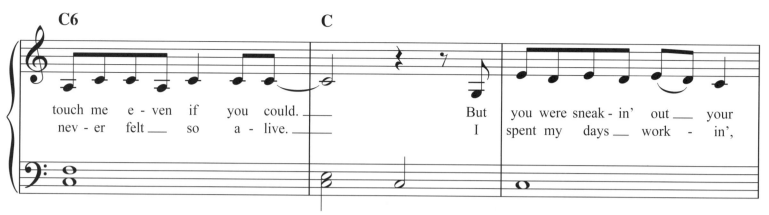

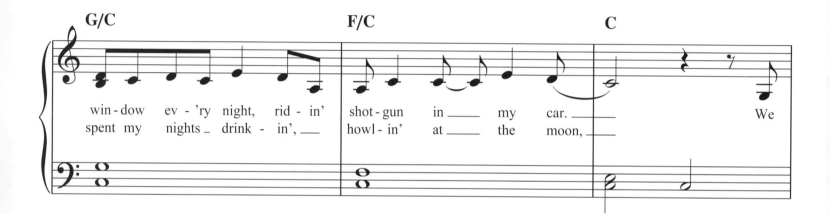

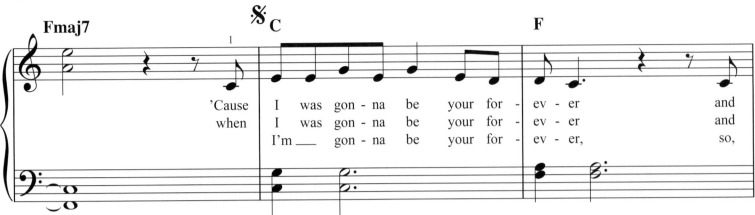

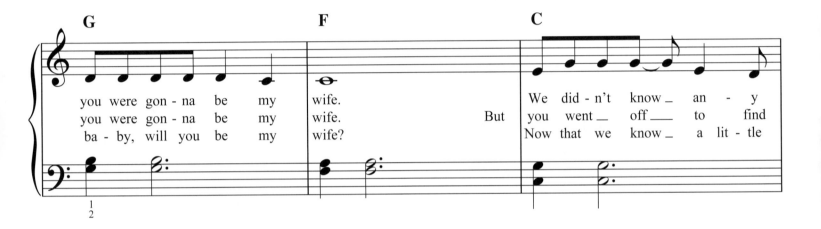

We were gon - na be the great - est love sto - ry this
We were gon - na be the great - est love sto - ry this
We're _ gon - na be the great - est love sto - ry this

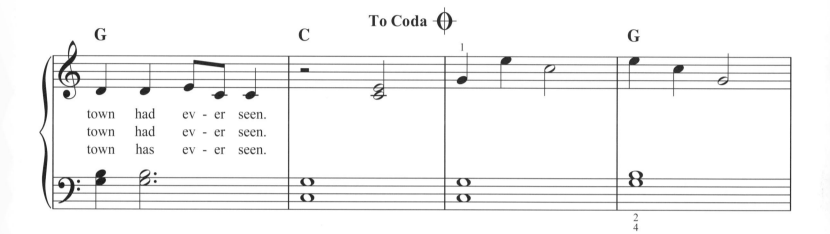

To Coda

town had ev - er seen.
town had ev - er seen.
town has ev - er seen.

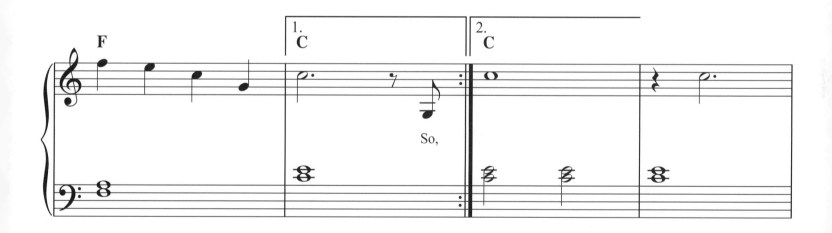

So,

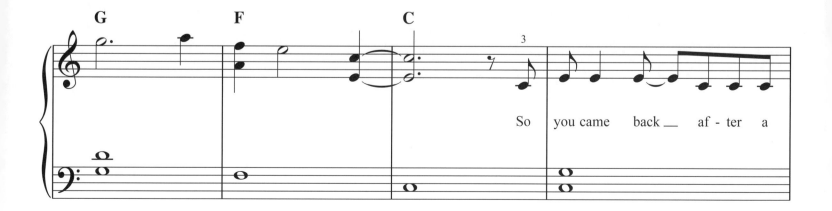

So you came back _ af - ter a

long four years. Your col-lege boy-friend did-n't work out. ___ So,

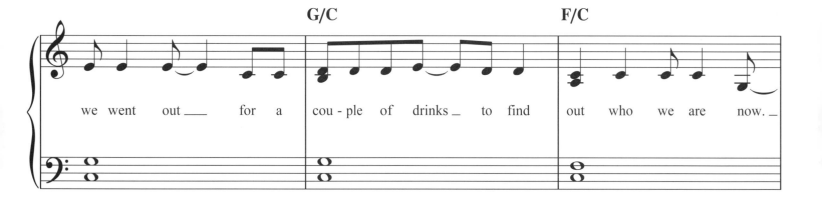

we went out ___ for a cou-ple of drinks ___ to find out who we are now. ___

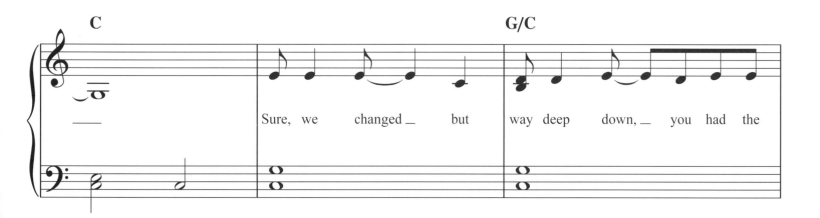

___ Sure, we changed ___ but way deep down, ___ you had the

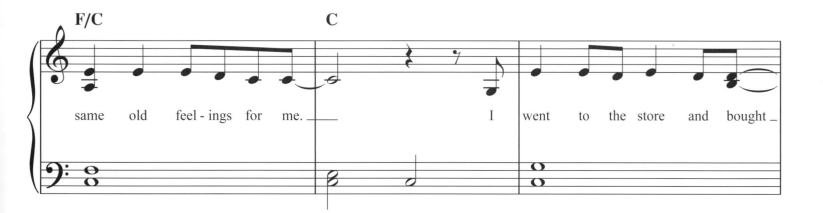

same old feel-ings for me. ___ I went to the store and bought ___

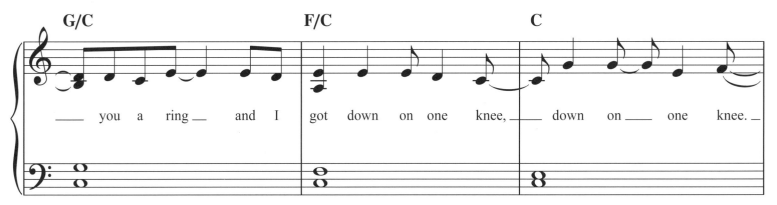

you a ring and I got down on one knee, down on one knee.

And I said:

CODA

We're gon-na be the great-est love sto-ry this world has ev-er seen.

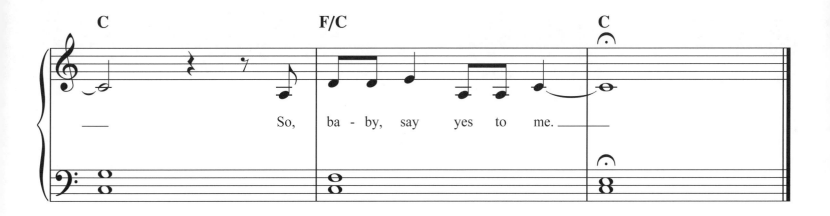

So, ba-by, say yes to me.

HALLELUJAH
featured in the DreamWorks Motion Picture SHREK

Words and Music by
LEONARD COHEN

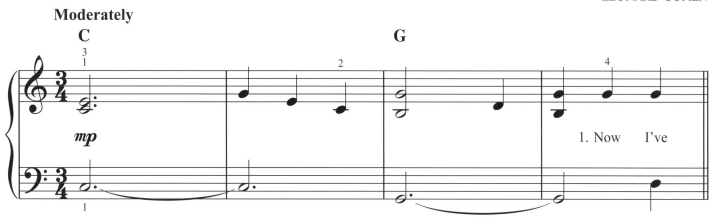

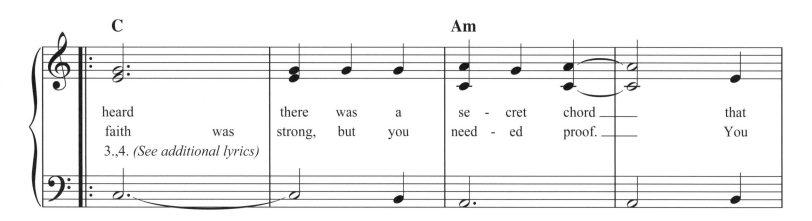

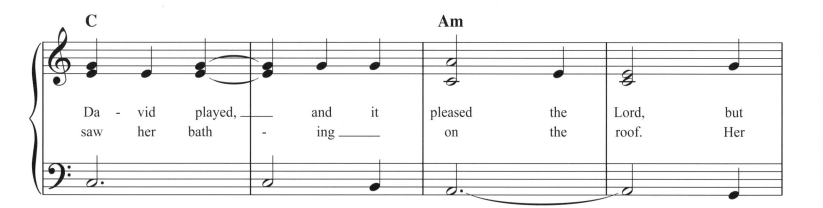

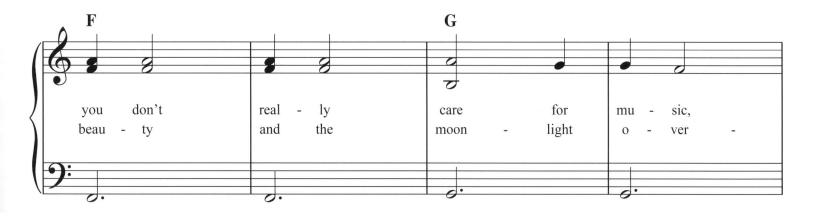

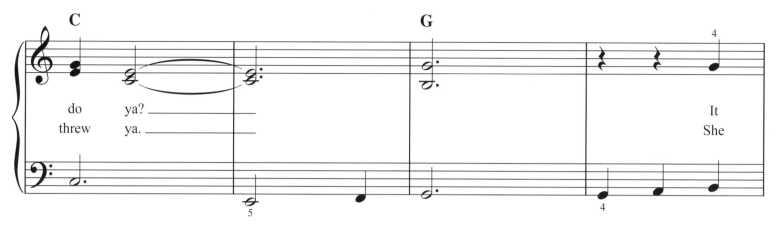

do ya? _____
threw ya. _____
It
She

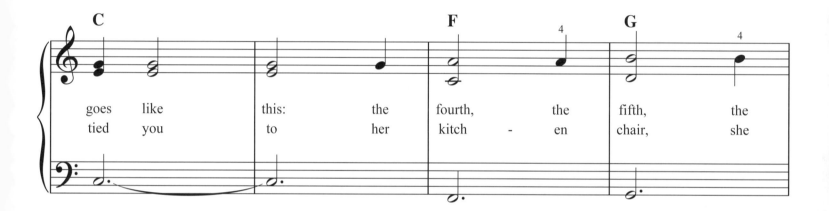

goes like   this: the fourth,   the fifth,   the
tied you   to her kitch - en chair, she

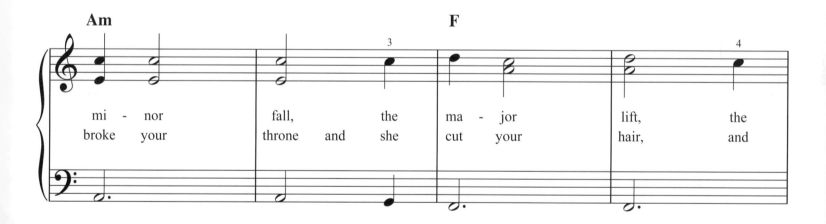

mi - nor fall, the ma - jor lift, the
broke your throne and she cut your hair, and

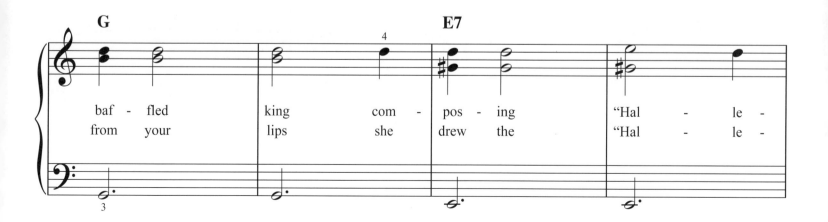

baf - fled king com - pos - ing "Hal - le -
from your lips she drew the "Hal - le -

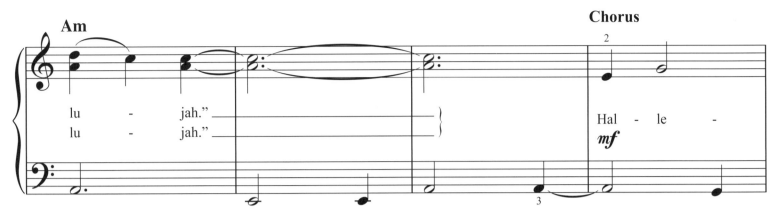

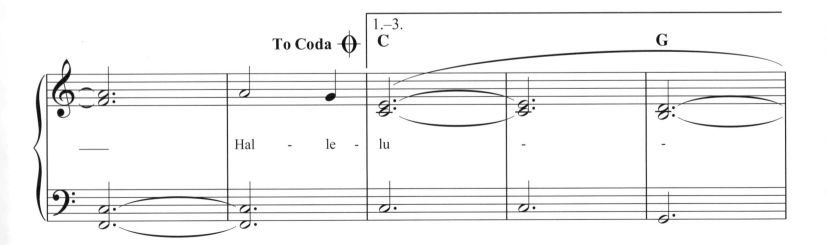

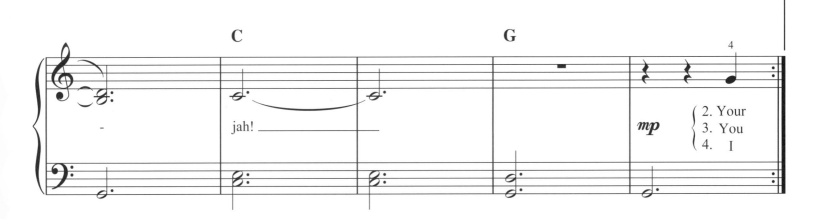

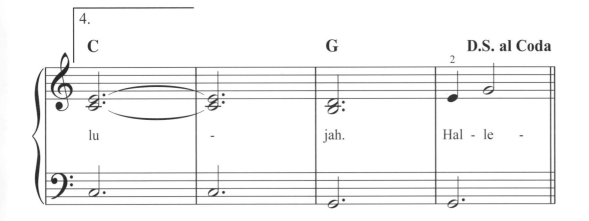

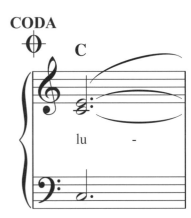

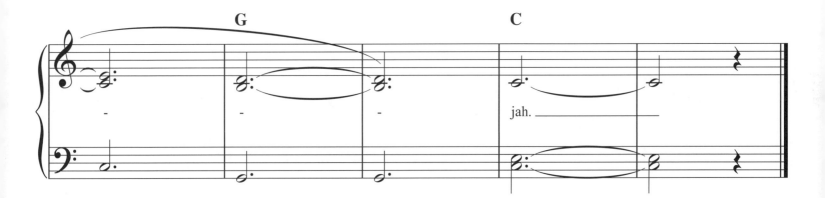

Additional Lyrics

3. You say I took the Name in vain:
   I don't even know the Name,
   But if I did, well, really, what's it to ya?
   There's a blaze of light in every word.
   It doesn't matter which are heard,
   The holy or the broken Hallelujah.
   Chorus

4. I did my best; it wasn't much.
   I couldn't feel, so I tried to touch.
   I've told the truth; I didn't come to fool ya.
   And even though it all went wrong,
   I'll stand before the Lord of Song
   With nothing on my tongue but "Hallelujah."
   Chorus

HAPPY
from DESPICABLE ME 2

Words and Music by
PHARRELL WILLIAMS

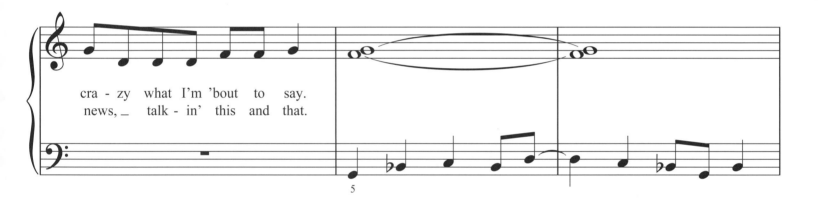

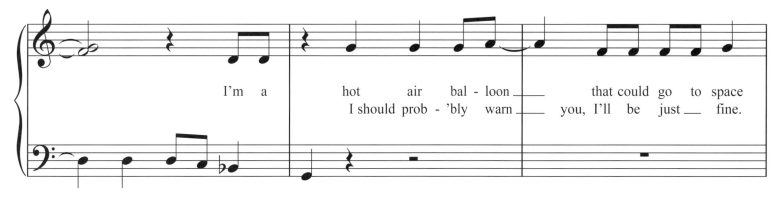

I'm a hot air bal - loon ____ that could go to space
I should prob - 'bly warn ____ you, I'll be just ___ fine.

with the air like I don't
No of - fense to

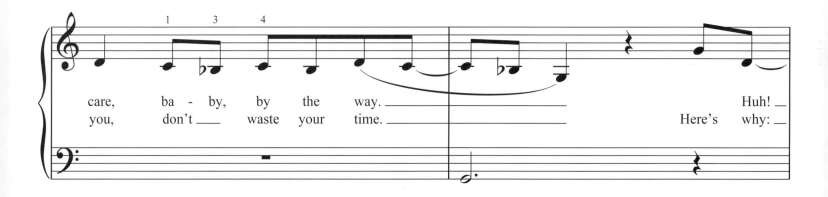

care, ba - by, by the way. ____ Huh!
you, don't ___ waste your time. ____ Here's why: ___

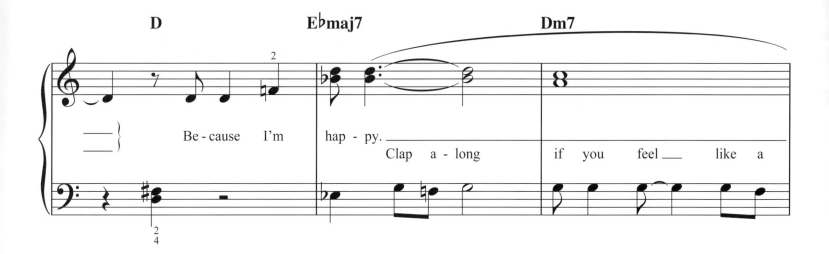

D   **E♭maj7**   **Dm7**

Be - cause I'm hap - py. ____
Clap a - long if you feel ___ like a

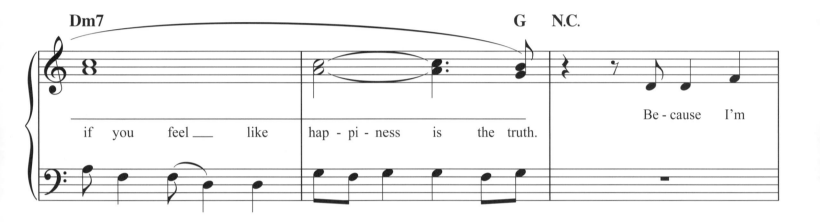

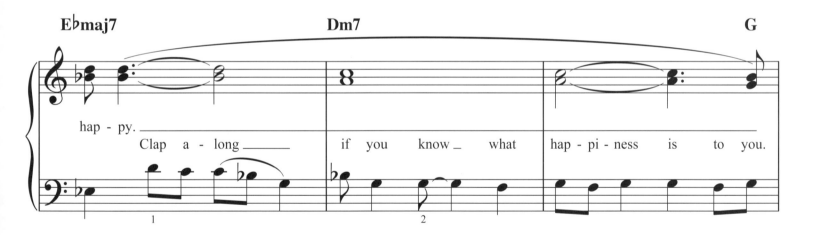

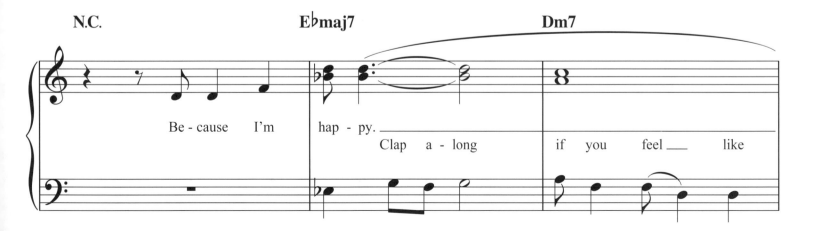

that's what you wan - na do. Bring me down, ___

___ can't noth - in' bring me down; ___ your love is too

high. Bring me down, ___ can't noth - in' bring me down. ___

___ (Let me tell you now.) Bring me down, ___ can't noth - in'

bring me down; ___ your love is too high. Bring me down, ___

___ can't noth - in' bring me down. ___ Be - cause I'm

E♭maj7 **Dm7** **G**

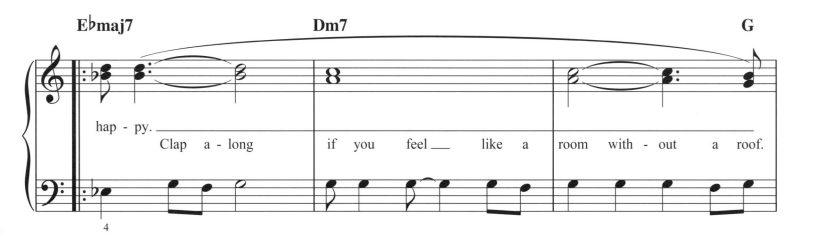

hap - py. ___
Clap a - long if you feel ___ like a room with - out a roof.

4

N.C. **E♭maj7** **Dm7**

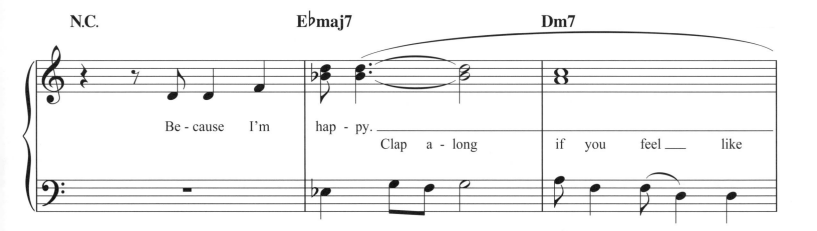

Be - cause I'm hap - py. ___
Clap a - long if you feel ___ like

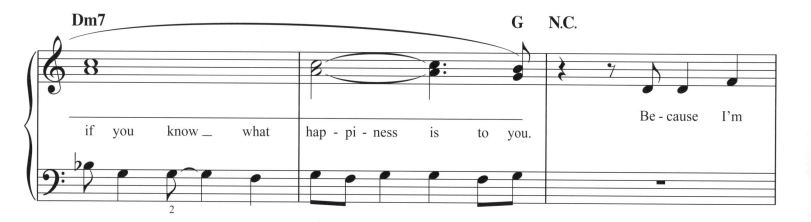

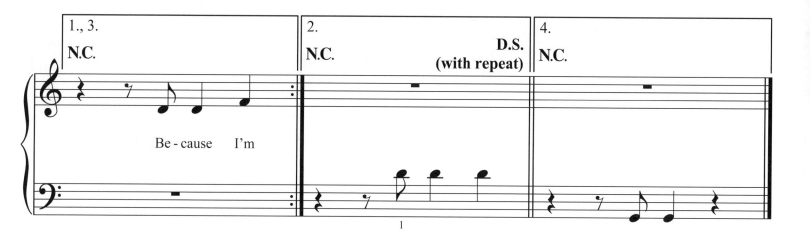

LOOK WHAT YOU MADE ME DO

Words and Music by TAYLOR SWIFT,
JACK ANTONOFF, RICHARD FAIRBRASS,
FRED FAIRBRASS and ROB MANZOLI

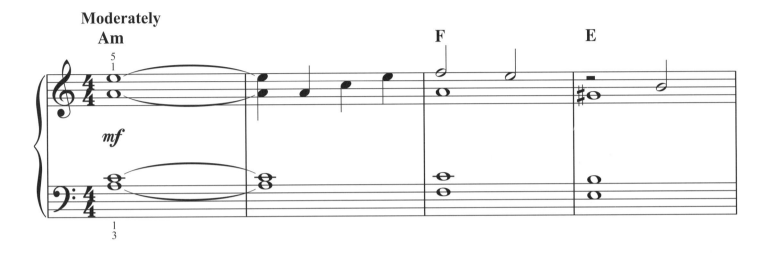

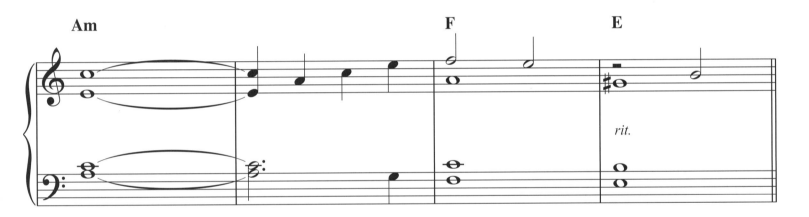

Urban Pop

I don't like your lit - tle games, don't

I don't like your per - fect crime, how

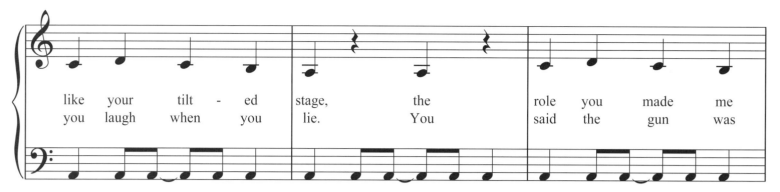

like your tilt - ed stage, the role you made me
you laugh when you lie. You said the gun was

play of the fool. No, I don't like you.
mine. Is-n't cool. No, I

don't like you.

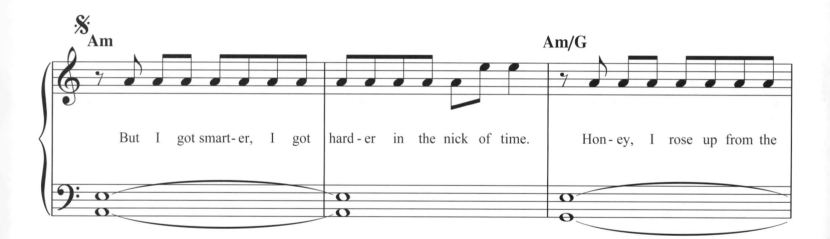

Am

But I got smart-er, I got hard-er in the nick of time.

Am/G

Hon-ey, I rose up from the

dead. I do it all the time.

F

I've got a list of names and yours is in red, un-der-lined,

keys, they once be - longed to me. You

asked me for a place to sleep, locked me out and threw a feast.

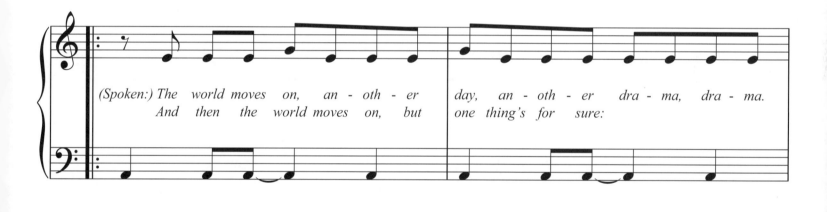

(Spoken:) The world moves on, an - oth - er day, an - oth - er dra - ma, dra - ma.
And then the world moves on, but one thing's for sure:

1. 2. **D.S. al Coda**

But not for me, not for me, all I think a - bout is kar - ma.
May - be I got mine, but you'll all get yours.

CODA

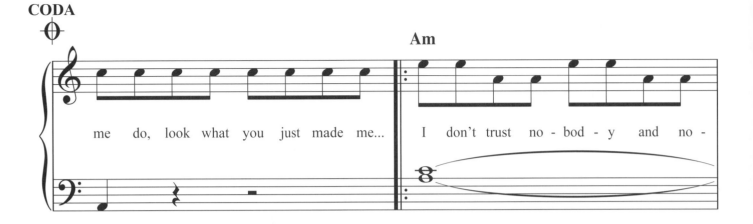

me do, look what you just made me... I don't trust no-bod-y and no-

bod-y trusts me. I'll be the ac-tress star-ring in your bad dreams.

star-ring in your bad dreams. I don't trust no-bod-y and no-bod-y trusts me.

I'll be the ac-tress star-ring in your bad dreams. star-ring in your bad dreams.

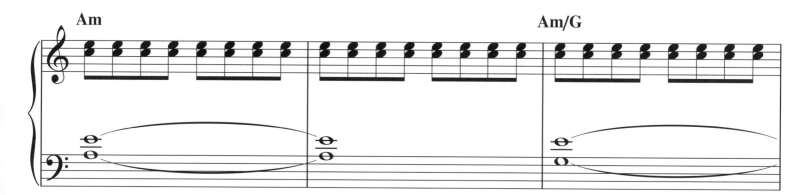

52

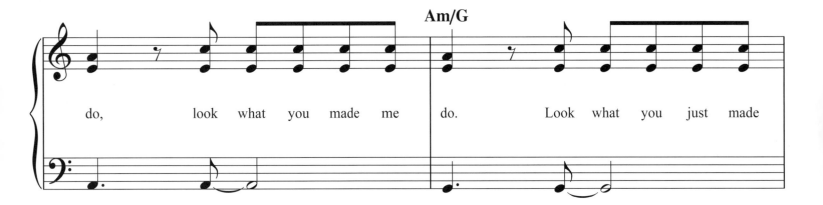

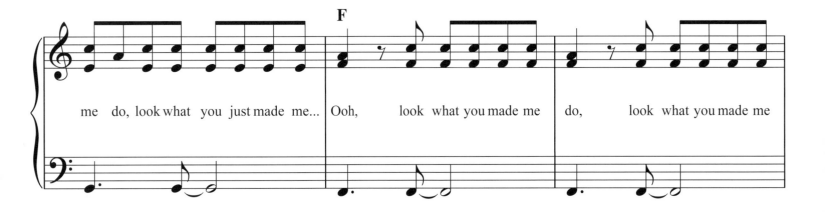

HAVANA

Words and Music by CAMILA CABELLO, LOUIS BELL,
PHARRELL WILLIAMS, ADAM FEENEY, ALI TAMPOSI,
BRIAN LEE, ANDREW WOTMAN, BRITTANY HAZZARD,
JEFFERY LAMAR WILLIAMS and KAAN GUNESBERK

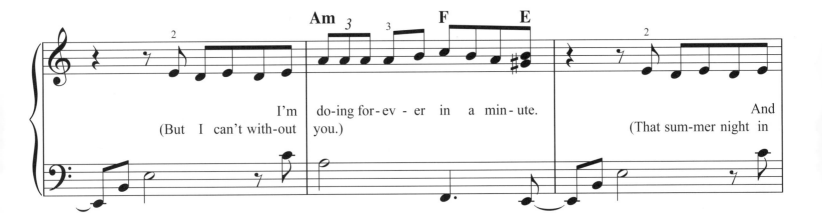

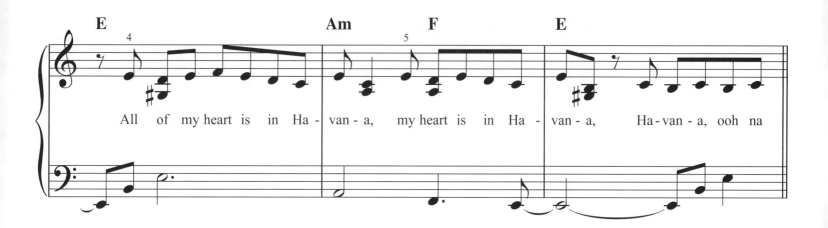

Ooh na na na, ooh na na na. Take me back, back, back. Ooh na na na, ooh na na

1.
na. Take me back, back, back.

2.
na. Take me back, back, back.

Trumpet solo

Ooh.

Ooh.

Ha - van - a, ooh na na.

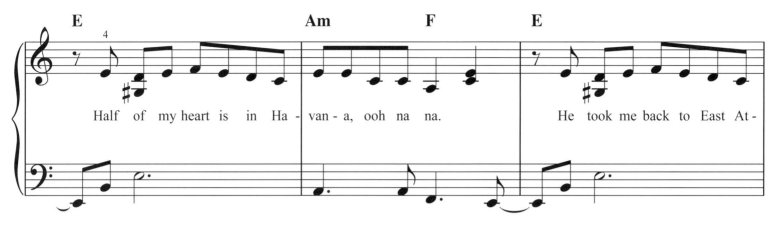

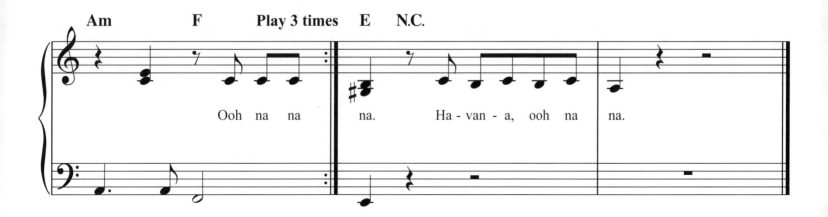

HELLO

Words and Music by ADELE ADKINS
and GREG KURSTIN

Moderately

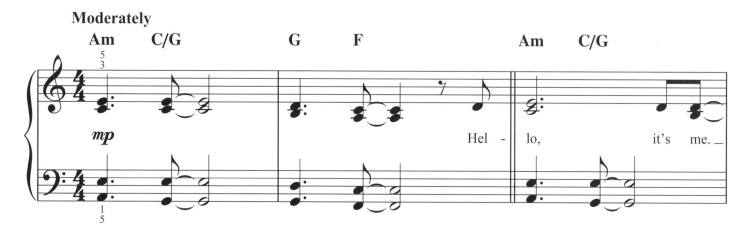

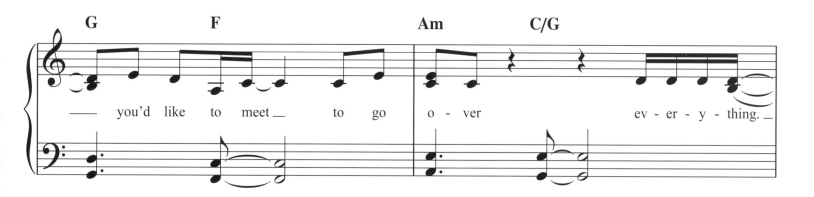

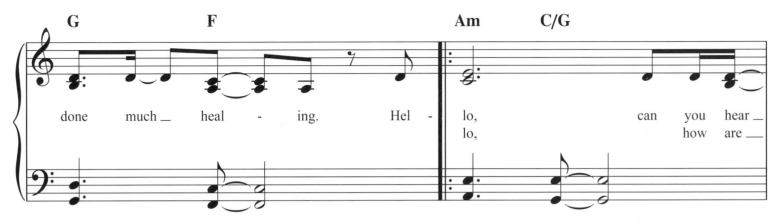

done much _ heal - ing. Hel - lo, _ can you hear _
lo, _ how are _

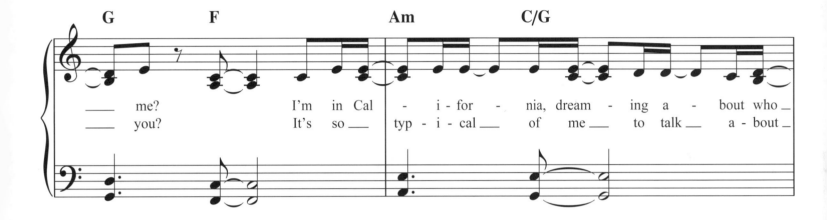

_ me? I'm in Cal - i - for - nia, dream - ing a - bout who _
_ you? It's so _ typ - i - cal _ of me _ to talk _ a - bout _

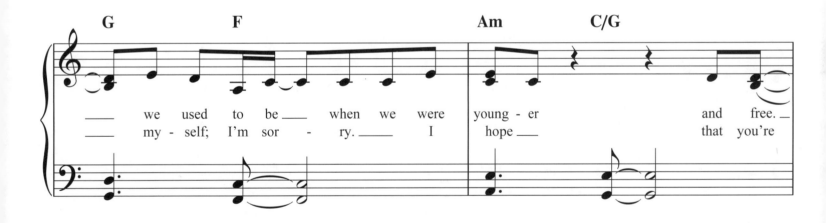

_ we used to be _ when we were young - er and free. _
_ my - self; I'm sor - ry. _ I hope _ that you're

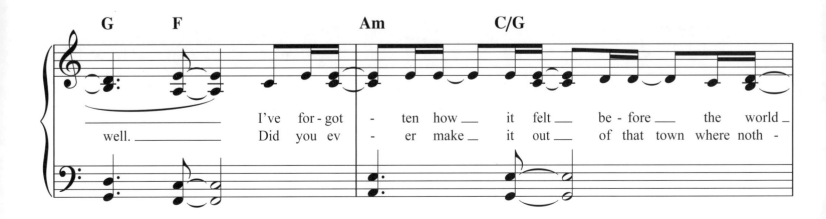

_ well. _ I've for - got - ten how _ it felt _ be - fore _ the world _
well. _ Did you ev - er make _ it out _ of that town where noth -

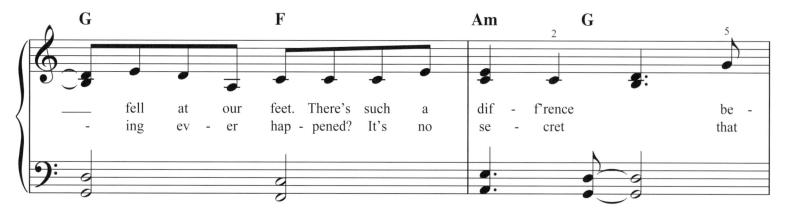

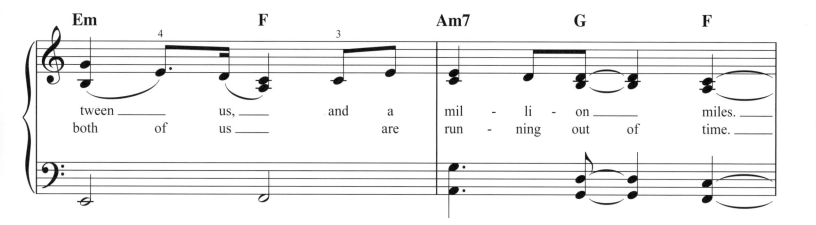

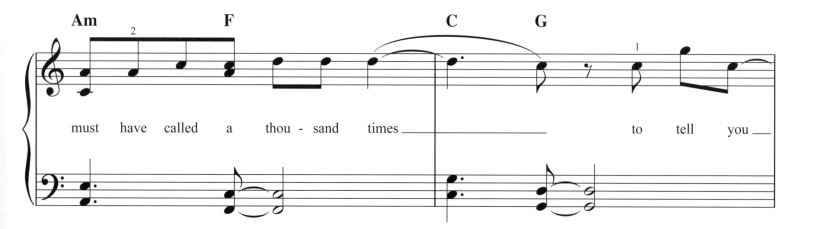

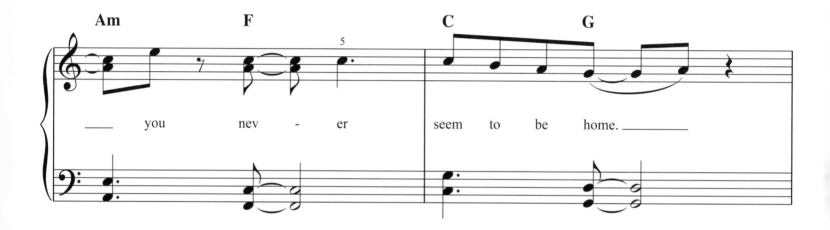

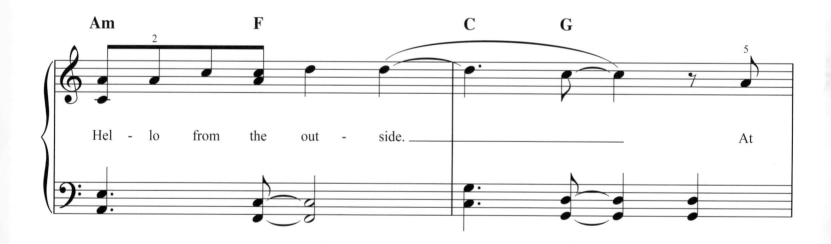

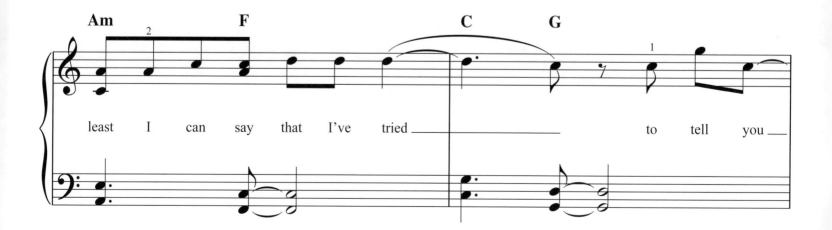

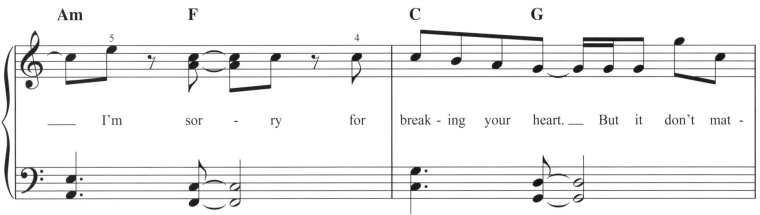

Am   **F**   **C**   **G**

I'm sor - ry for break - ing your heart.__ But it don't mat -

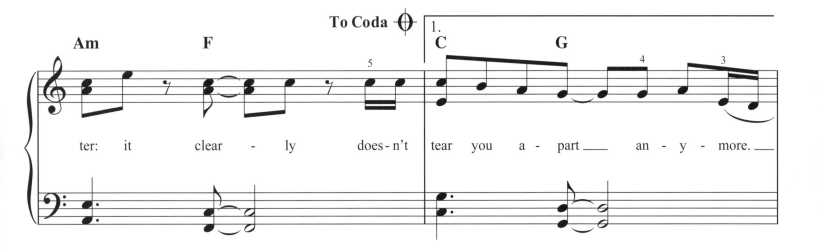

To Coda ⊕   1.

Am   **F**   **C**   **G**

ter: it clear - ly does - n't tear you a - part__ an - y - more.__

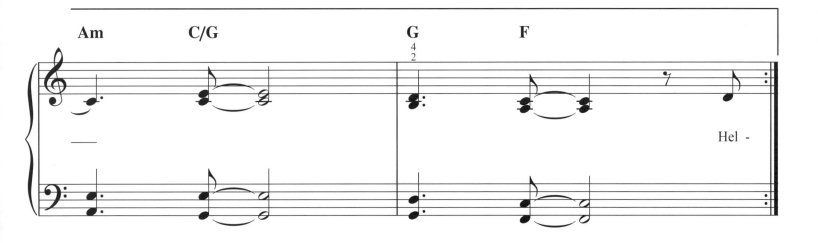

Am   **C/G**   **G**   **F**

__ Hel -

2.

C   **G**   **Am**   **F**

tear you a - part__ an - y - more.__

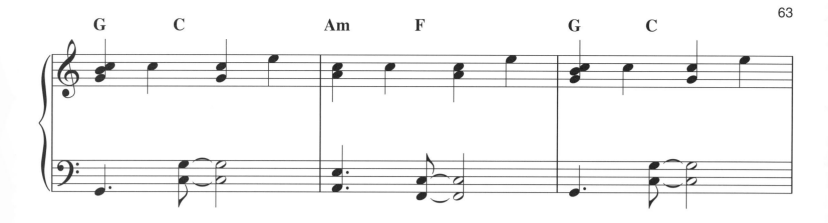

THE MIDDLE

Words and Music by SARAH AARONS,
MARCUS LOMAX, JORDAN JOHNSON,
ANTON ZASLAVSKI, KYLE TREWARTHA,
MICHAEL TREWARTHA and STEFAN JOHNSON

Moderately fast

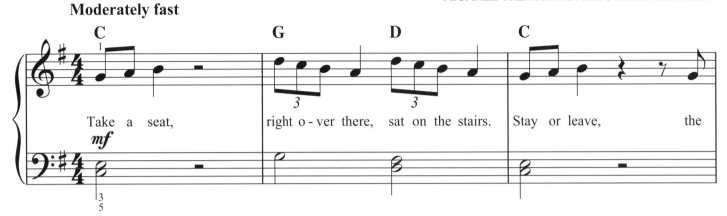

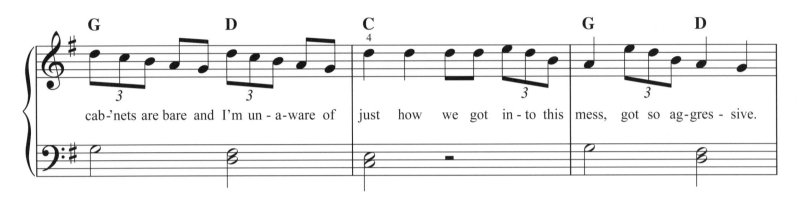

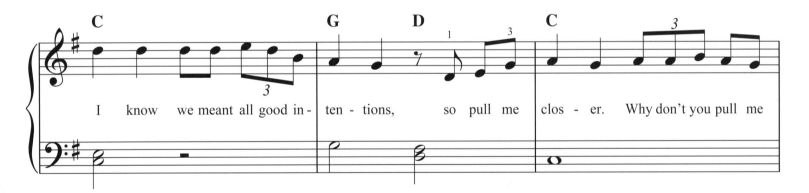

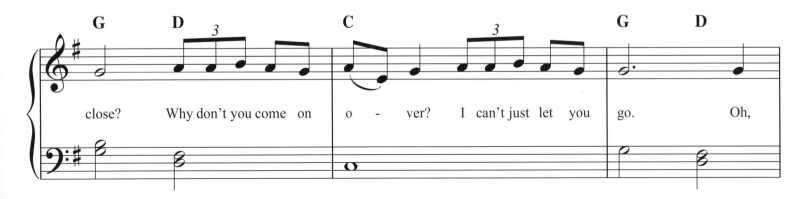

ba - by,   why don't you just meet me   in the   mid - dle?   I'm

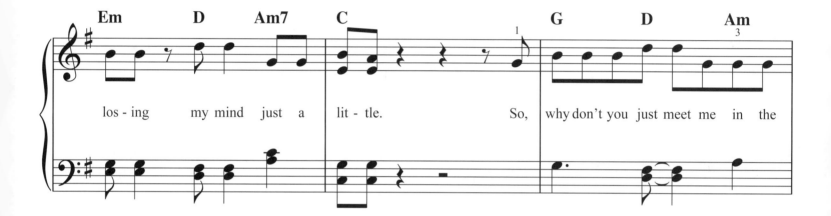

los - ing   my mind just a   lit - tle.   So, why don't you just meet me   in the

mid - dle,   in the   mid - dle?   Ba - by,

why don't you just meet me   in the   mid - dle?   I'm los - ing   my mind just a

lit - tle.   So, why don't you just meet me in the mid - dle,   in the

mid - dle?   Take a step   back for a min - ute, in - to the kit - chen,

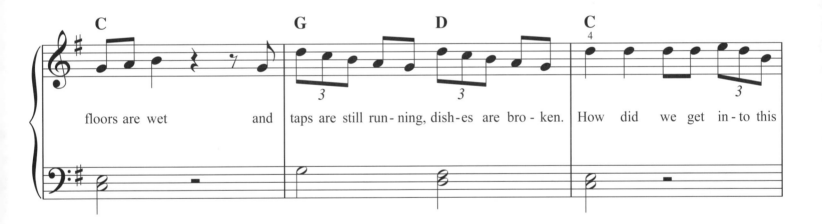

floors are wet   and taps are still run - ning, dish-es are bro - ken. How did we get in - to this

mess, got so ag-gres - sive.   I know we meant all good in - ten - tions,   so pull me

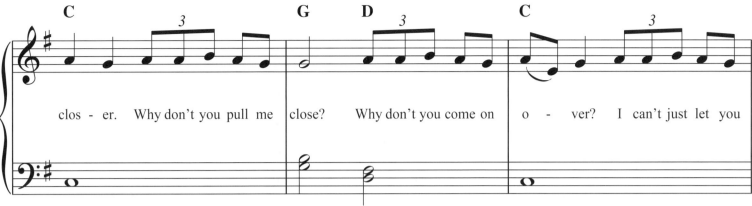

clos - er. Why don't you pull me close? Why don't you come on o - ver? I can't just let you

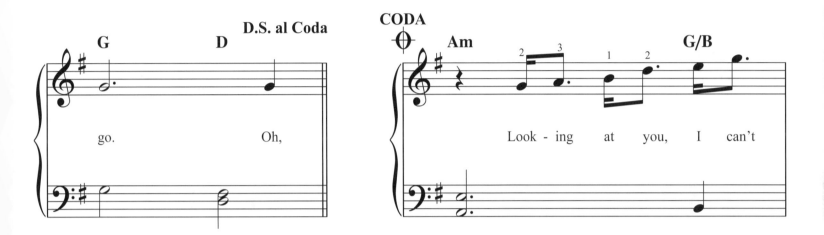

go. Oh, Look - ing at you, I can't

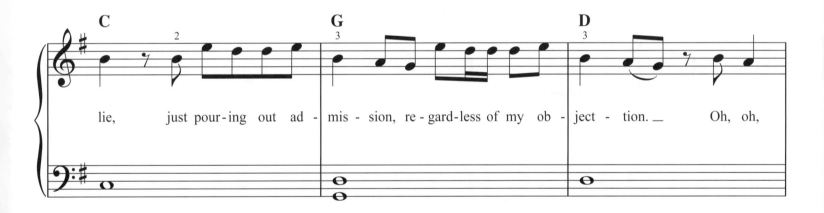

lie, just pour-ing out ad - mis - sion, re - gard-less of my ob - ject - tion. ___ Oh, oh,

and it's not a - bout my pride, I need you on my skin, just ___ come o - ver, pull me

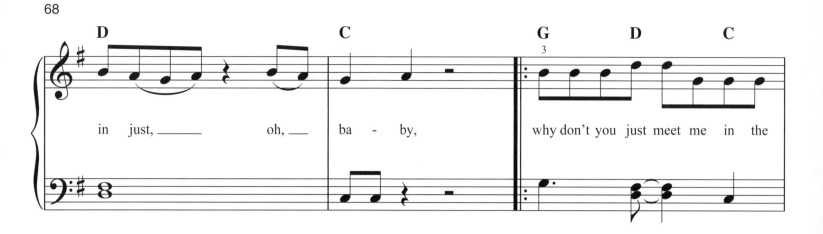

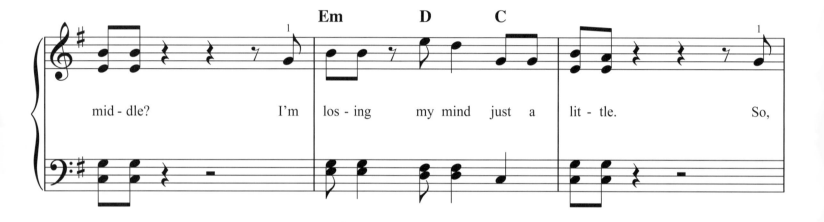

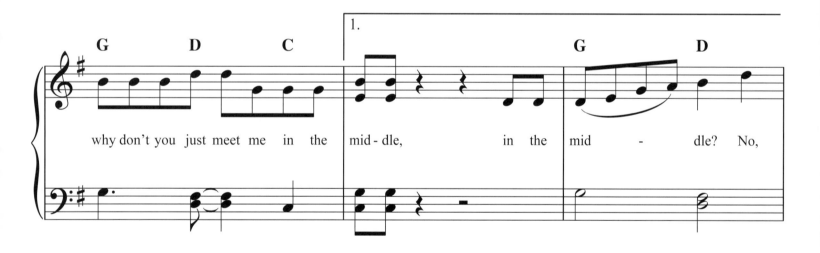

MY SHOT
from HAMILTON

Words and Music by
LIN-MANUEL MIRANDA
with ALBERT JOHNSON, KEJUAN WALIEK MUCHITA,
OSTEN HARVEY, JR., ROGER TROUTMAN,
CHRISTOPHER WALLACE

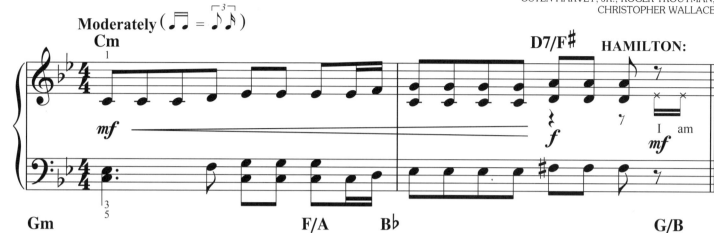

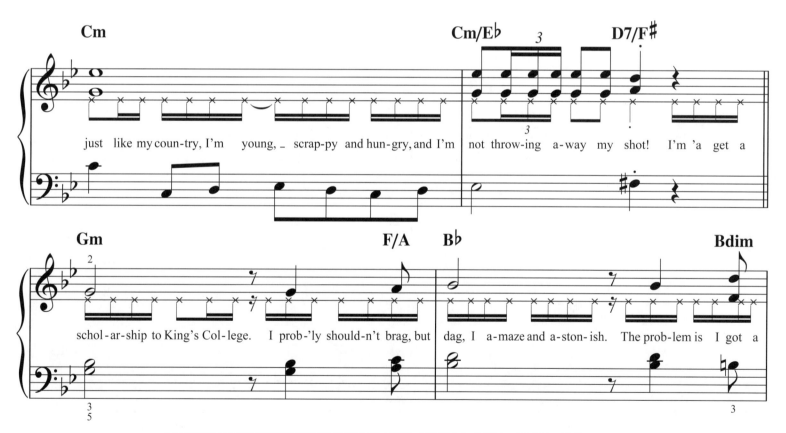

lot of brains but no pol-ish.   I got-ta hol-ler just to be heard. With ev-er-y word, __ I drop know-edge! I'm a

dia-mond in the rough,   a shin-y piece of coal tryin' to reach my goal. My pow-er of speech: un-im-peach-a-ble.

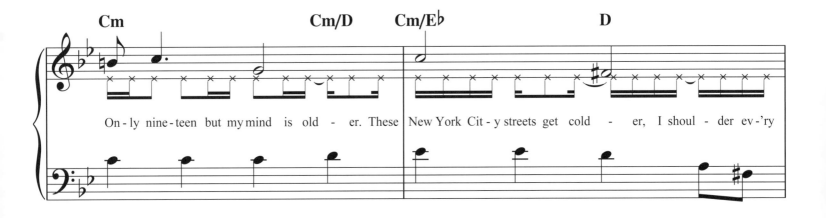

On-ly nine-teen but my mind is old - er. These New York Cit-y streets get cold - er, I shoul-der ev'ry

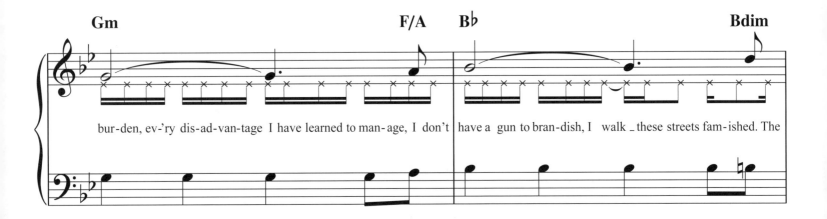

bur-den, ev'ry dis-ad-van-tage I have learned to man-age, I don't have a gun to bran-dish, I walk __ these streets fam-ished. The

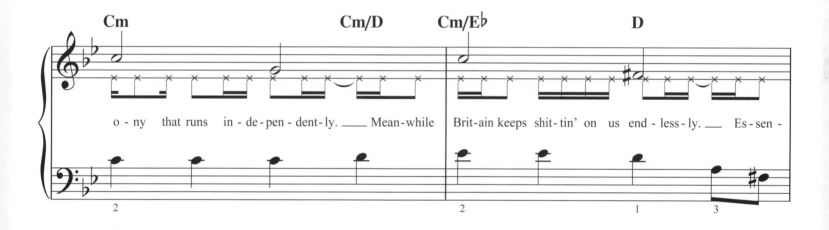

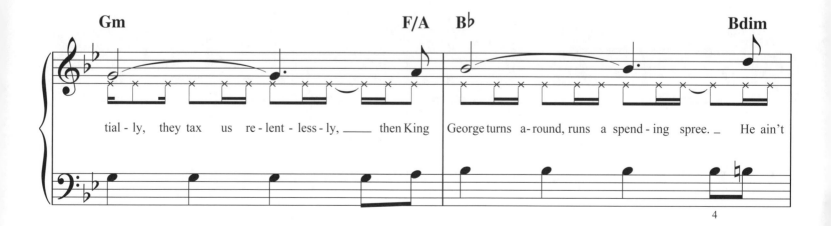

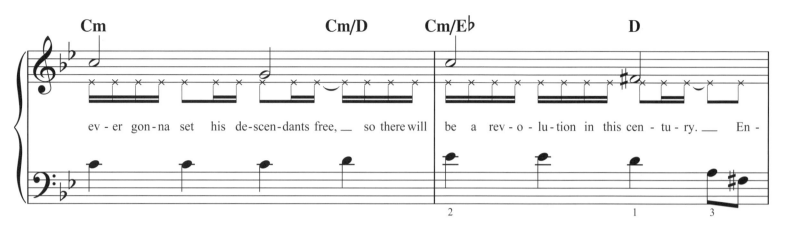

Cm   **Cm/D**   **Cm/Eb**   **D**

ev - er gon-na set his de-scen-dants free, __ so there will be a rev-o-lu-tion in this cen-tu-ry. __ En -

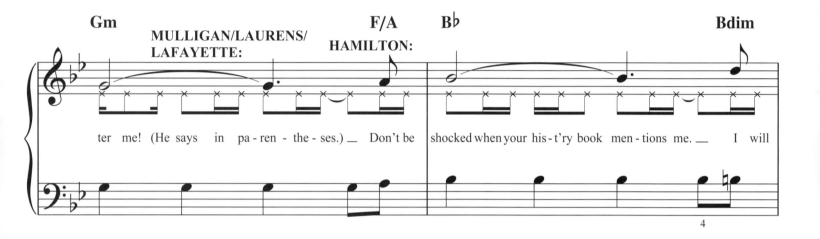

Gm   **F/A**   **Bb**   **Bdim**

MULLIGAN/LAURENS/LAFAYETTE: HAMILTON:

ter me! (He says in pa-ren-the-ses.) __ Don't be shocked when your his-t'ry book men-tions me. __ I will

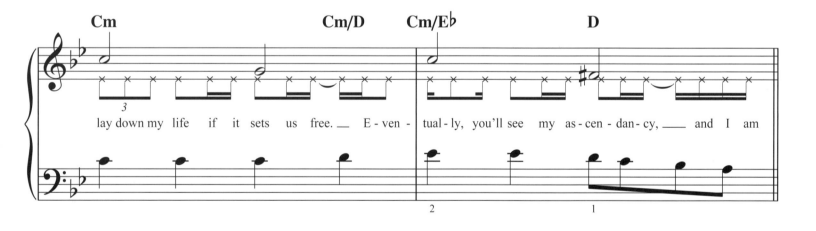

Cm   **Cm/D**   **Cm/Eb**   **D**

lay down my life if it sets us free. __ E-ven-tual-ly, you'll see my as-cen-dan-cy, ___ and I am

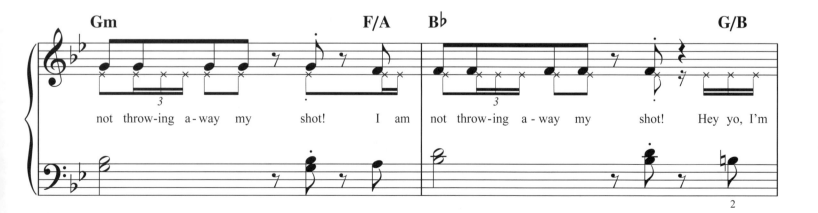

Gm   **F/A**   **Bb**   **G/B**

not throw-ing a-way my shot! I am not throw-ing a-way my shot! Hey yo, I'm

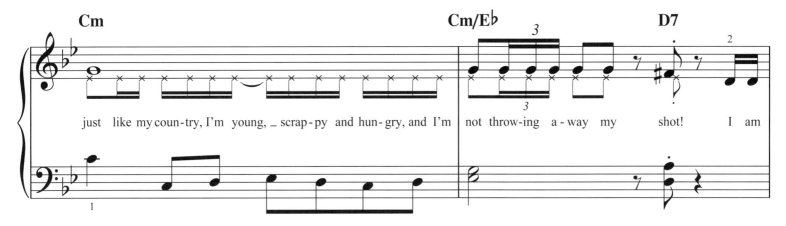

Cm   **Cm/E♭**   **D7**

just like my coun-try, I'm young, _ scrap-py and hun-gry, and I'm not throw-ing a-way my shot! I am

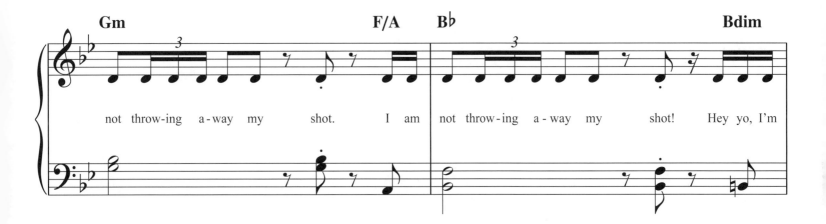

Gm   **F/A**   **B♭**   **Bdim**

not throw-ing a-way my shot. I am not throw-ing a-way my shot! Hey yo, I'm

Cm   **Cm/E♭**   **D7/F♯**

just like my coun-try, I'm young, _ scrap-py and hun-gry, and I'm not throw-ing a-way my shot. Ev-'ry-bod-y sing:

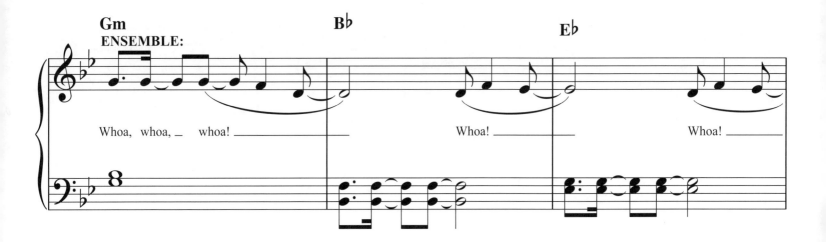

Gm   **B♭**   **E♭**

ENSEMBLE:

Whoa, whoa, _ whoa! _____ Whoa! _____ Whoa! _____

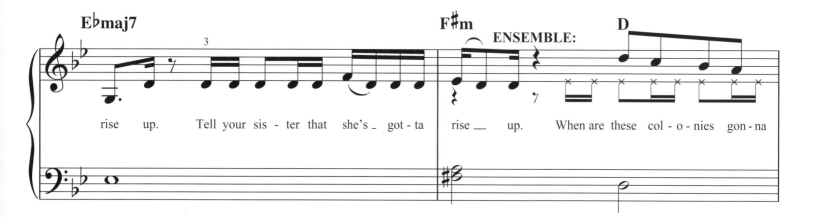

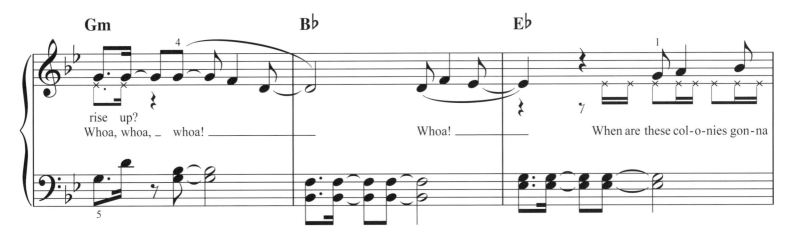

rise up?
Whoa, whoa, _ whoa! _____ Whoa! _____ When are these col-o-nies gon-na

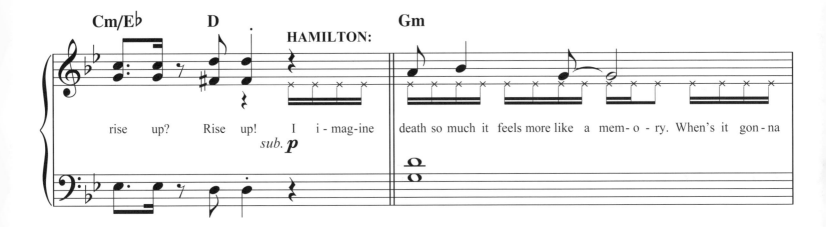

HAMILTON:

rise up? Rise up! I i-mag-ine death so much it feels more like a mem-o-ry. When's it gon-na

sub. **p**

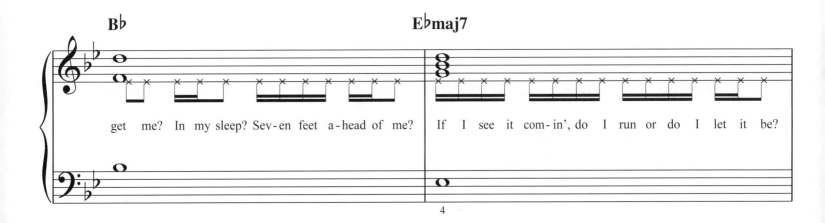

get me? In my sleep? Sev-en feet a-head of me? If I see it com-in', do I run or do I let it be?

Is it like a beat with-out a mel-o-dy? See, I nev-er thought I'd live past twen-ty. Where I come from

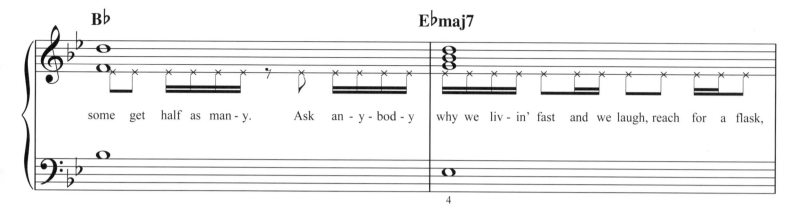

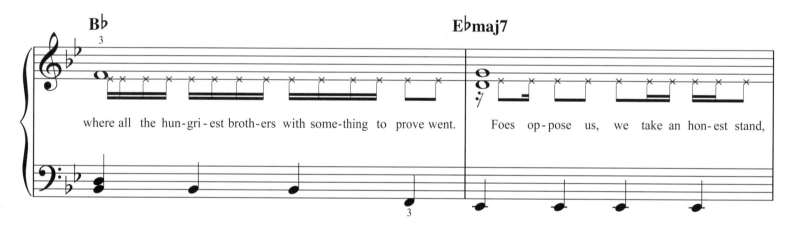

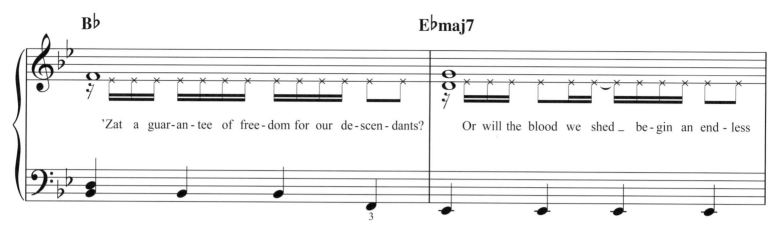

'Zat a guar-an-tee of free-dom for our de-scen-dants? Or will the blood we shed be-gin an end-less

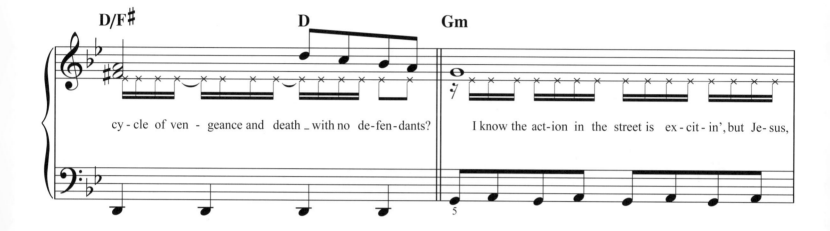

cy-cle of ven-geance and death with no de-fen-dants? I know the act-ion in the street is ex-cit-in', but Je-sus,

be-tween all the bleed-in' 'n' fight-in' I've been read-in' 'n' writ-in'. We need to han-dle our fi-nan-cial sit-u-a-tion.

Are we a na-tion of states? What's the state of our na-tion? I'm past pa-tient-ly wait-in'. I'm pas-sion-ate-ly smash-in'

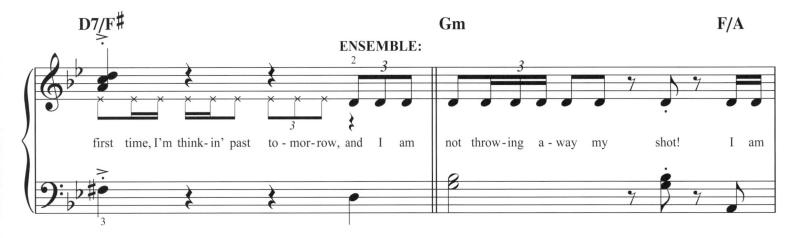

Not throw-ing a-way my shot! We're gon-na rise up! Rise ___ up!
It's time to take a shot!

Rise ___ up! Rise ___ up! It's time to take a shot! Whoa, whoa, ___ whoa! ___

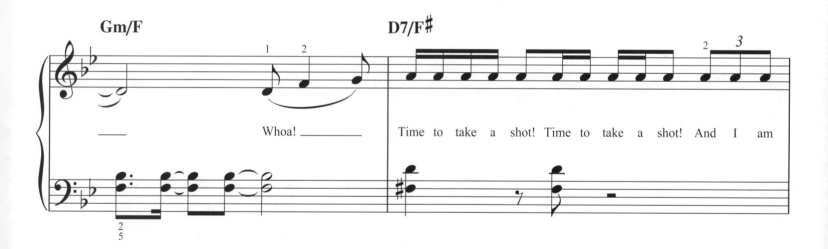

___ Whoa! ___ Time to take a shot! Time to take a shot! And I am

not throw-ing a-way my, not throw-ing a-way my shot!

PERFECT

Words and Music by
ED SHEERAN

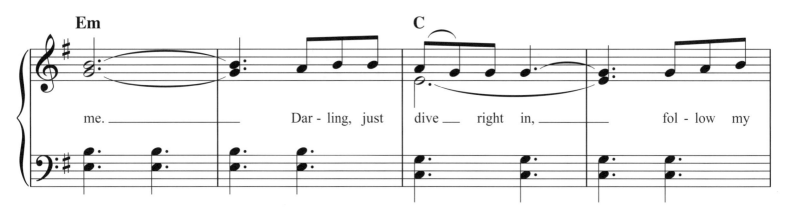

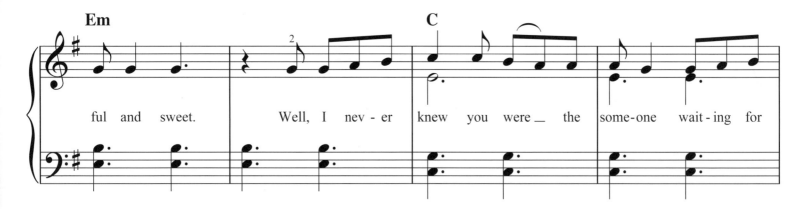

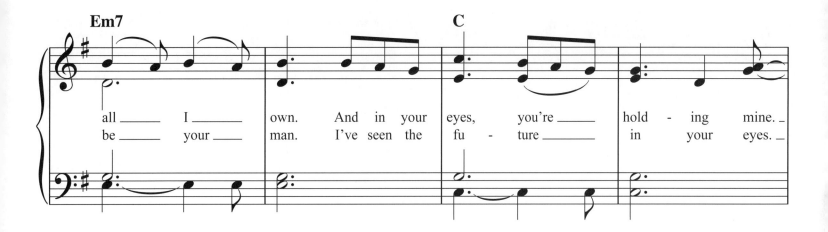

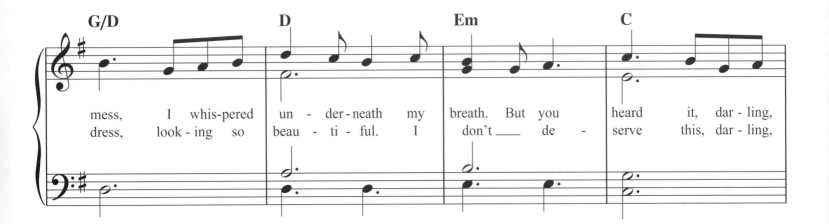

83

you look per - fect to - night.
you look per - fect to - night.

Well, I found a wom - an, strong - er than

an - y - one I know. She shares my dreams, I hope that some-day, I'll share her

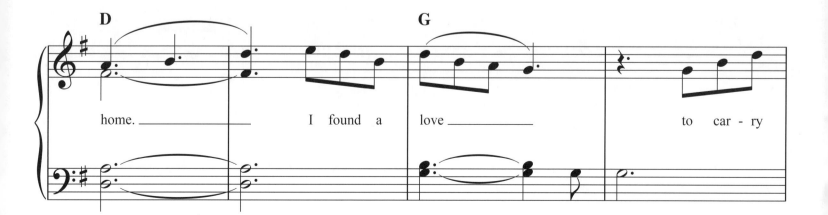

home. I found a love to car - ry

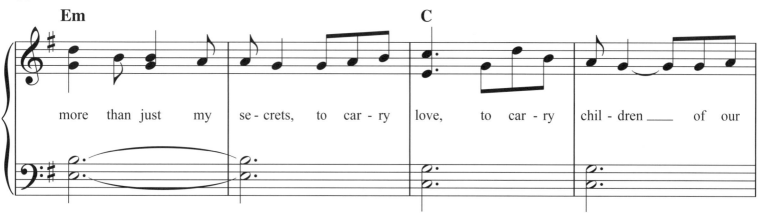

more than just my se - crets, to car - ry love, to car - ry chil - dren ____ of our

own. ____ We are still kids, but we're

D.S. al Coda

CODA

Ba - by, ____

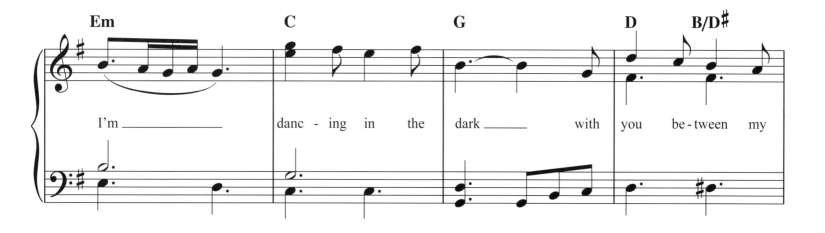

I'm ____ danc - ing in the dark ____ with you be - tween my

arms. Bare - foot on the grass, lis - ten - ing to our

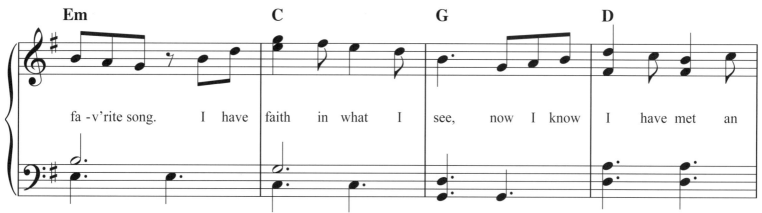

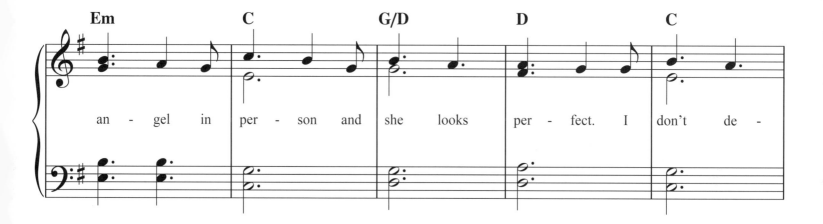

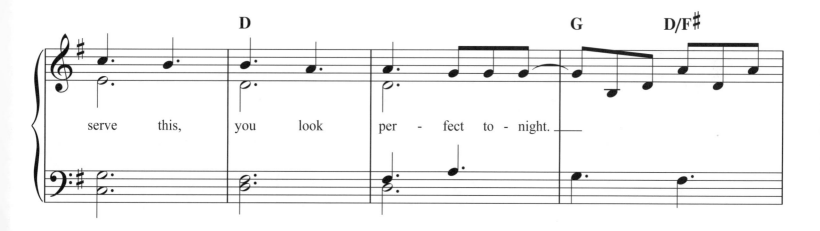

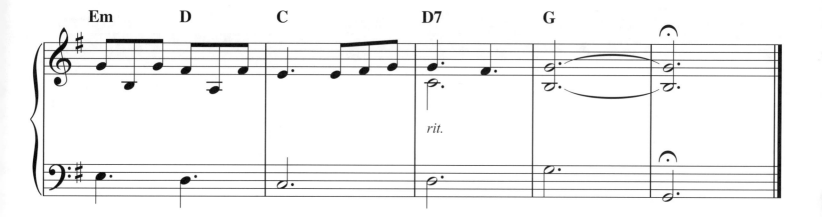

REMEMBER ME
(Ernesto de la Cruz)
from COCO

Music and Lyrics by KRISTEN ANDERSON-LOPEZ
and ROBERT LOPEZ

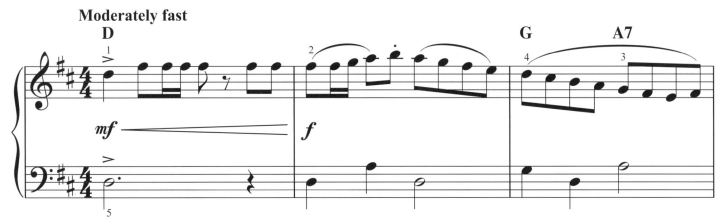

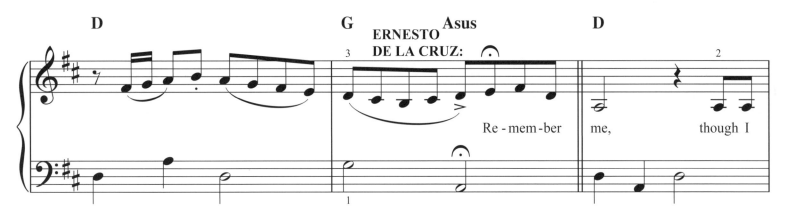

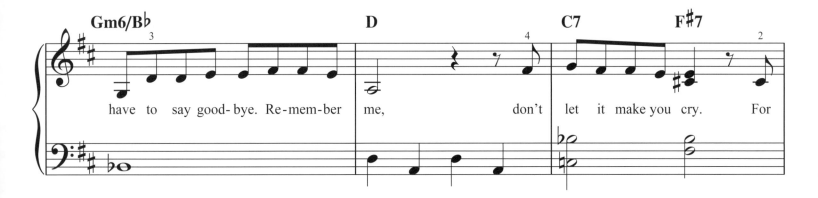

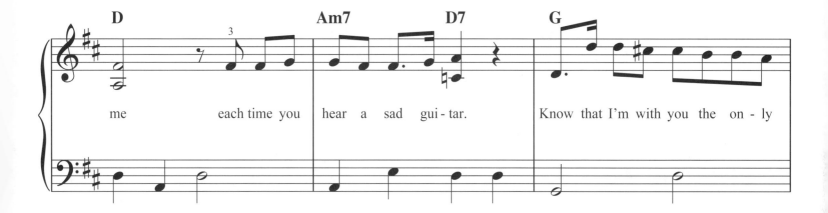

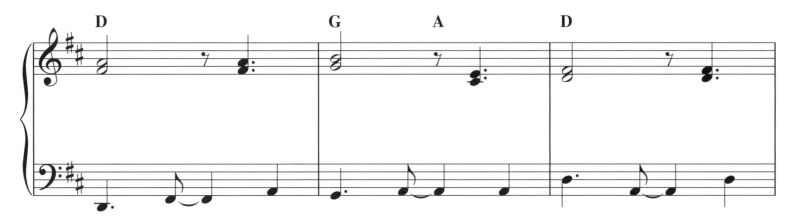

Re - mem - ber

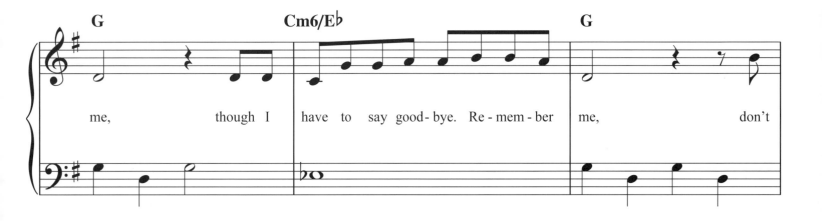

me,   though I have to say good-bye. Re - mem - ber   me,   don't

let it make you cry.   For   e - ven if I'm far a - way, __ I   hold you in my heart.   I

sing a se-cret song to you each night we are a-part. Re-mem - ber me though I

have to trav-el far. Re-mem-ber me each time you hear a sad gui-tar.

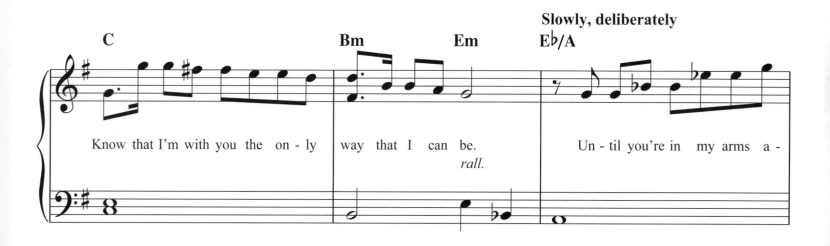

Know that I'm with you the on-ly way that I can be. *rall.* Un-til you're in my arms a-

Slowly, deliberately

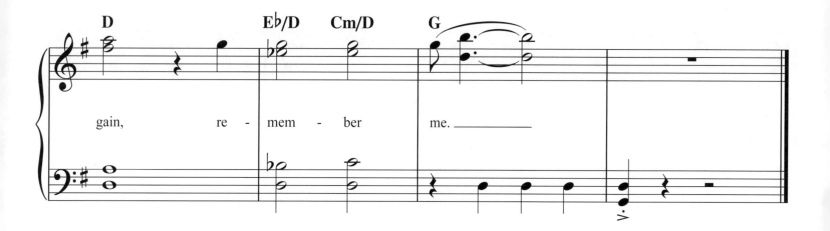

gain, re-mem - ber me. _____

REWRITE THE STARS
from THE GREATEST SHOWMAN

Words and Music by BENJ PASEK
and JUSTIN PAUL

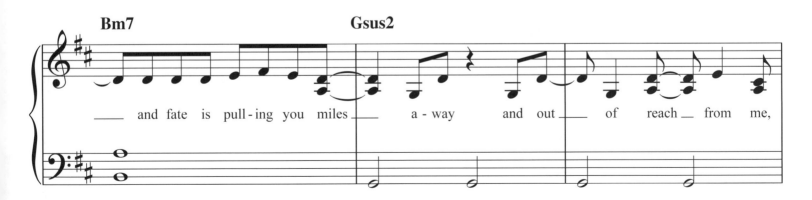

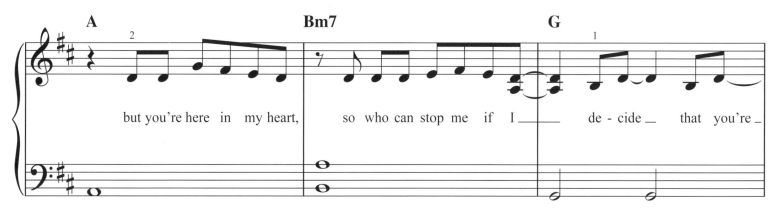

but you're here in my heart, so who can stop me if I ___ de - cide ___ that you're ___

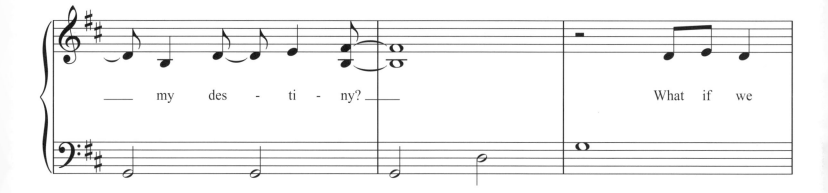

___ my des - ti - ny? ___ What if we

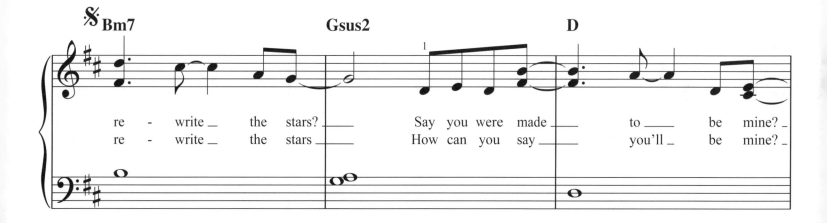

re - write ___ the stars? ___ Say you were made ___ to ___ be mine? ___
re - write ___ the stars ___ How can you say ___ you'll ___ be mine? ___

___ Noth - ing could keep us ___ a - part ___ You'd be the one ___
___ Ev - 'ry - thing keeps us ___ a - part ___ I'm not the one ___

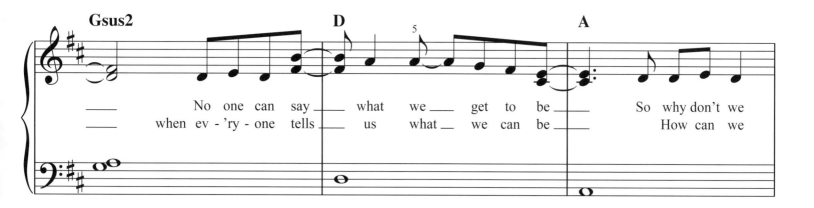

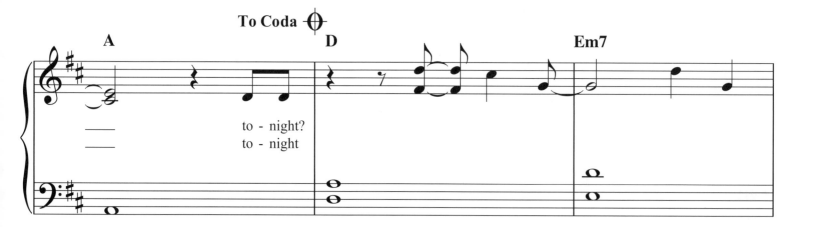

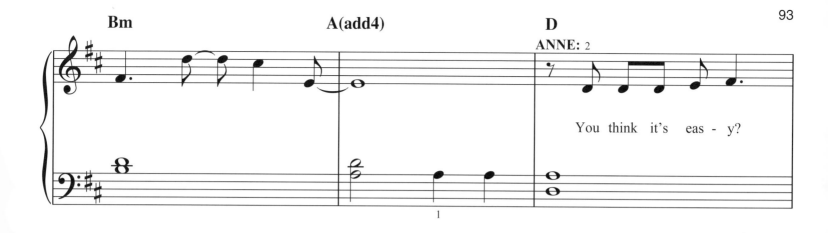

ANNE:

You think it's eas - y?

You think I don't want to run ____ to you? ___

But there are moun - tains, _____ and there are doors that we can't ___

___ walk through   I know you're won - der - in' why,   be - cause we're a - ble to be ___

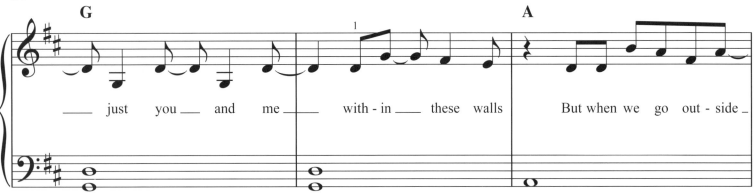

just you — and me — with-in — these walls But when we go out-side —

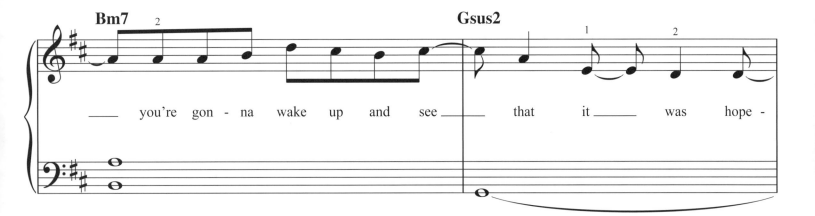

— you're gon - na wake up and see — that it — was hope -

D.S. al Coda

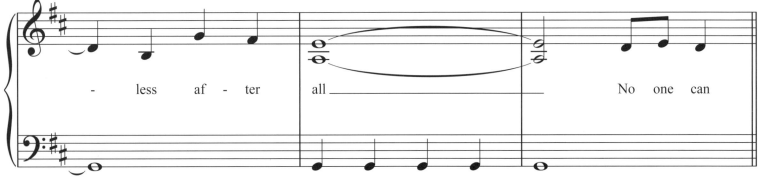

- less af - ter all — No one can

All I want is to fly — with you — All I want is to fall —

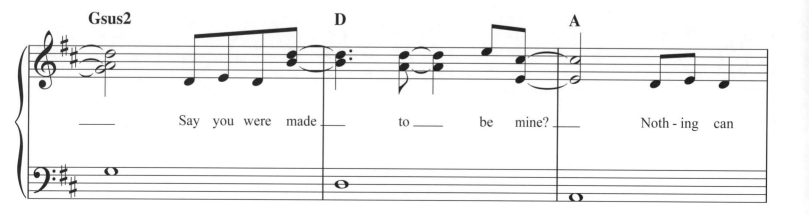

keep us ___ a - part ___ 'cause you are the one ___ I was meant ___ to find ___

___ It's up to you ___ and it's up to me ___ No one can say ___

___ what we ___ get to be ___ Why don't we re - write ___ the stars? ___

___ chang - in' the world ___ to ___ be ours? ___

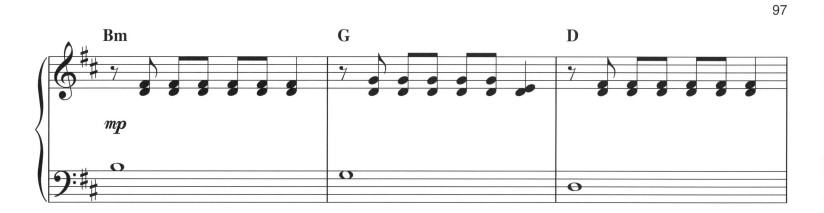

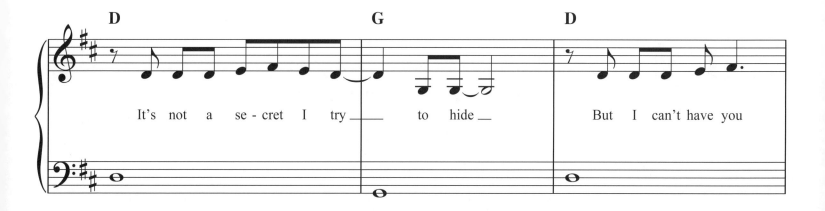

RISE UP

Words and Music by CASSANDRA BATIE
and JENNIFER DECILVEO

Slow Piano Ballad

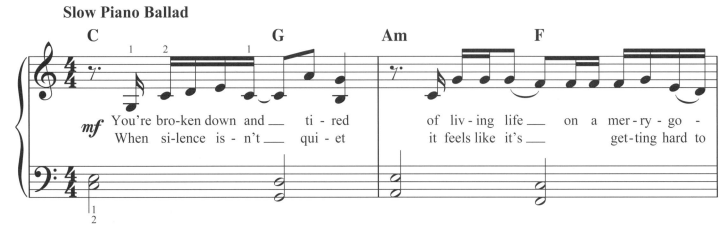

mf You're bro-ken down and __ ti-red
When si-lence is-n't __ qui-et

of liv-ing life __ on a mer-ry-go-
it feels like it's __ get-ting hard to

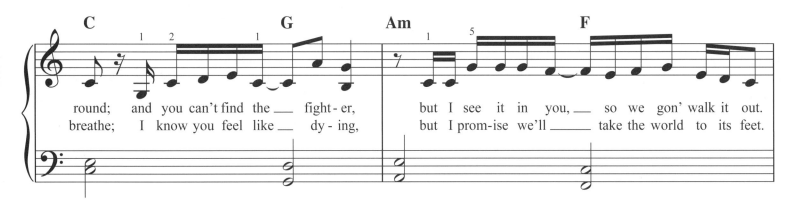

round; and you can't find the __ fight-er,
breathe; I know you feel like __ dy-ing,

but I see it in you, __ so we gon' walk it out.
but I prom-ise we'll _____ take the world to its feet.

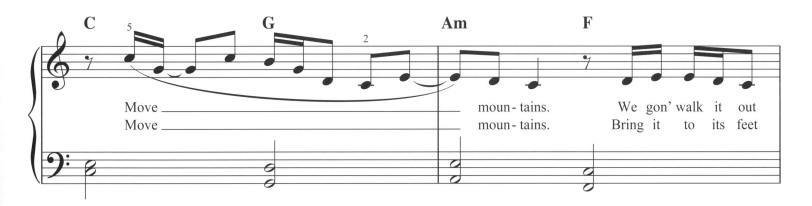

Move _____ moun-tains. We gon' walk it out
Move _____ moun-tains. Bring it to its feet

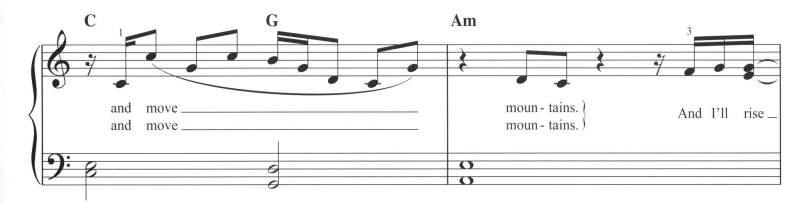

and move _____ moun-tains.
and move _____ moun-tains.

And I'll rise __

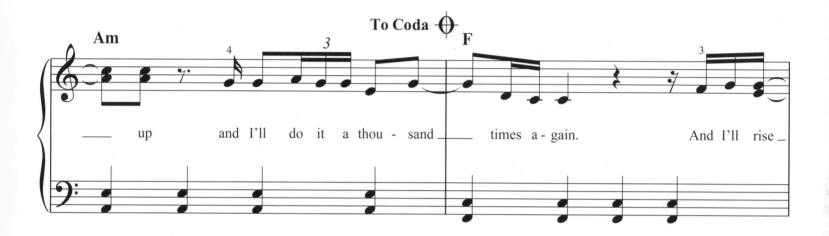

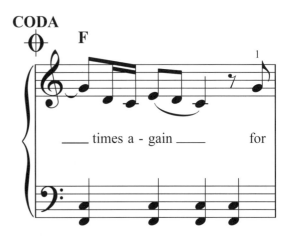

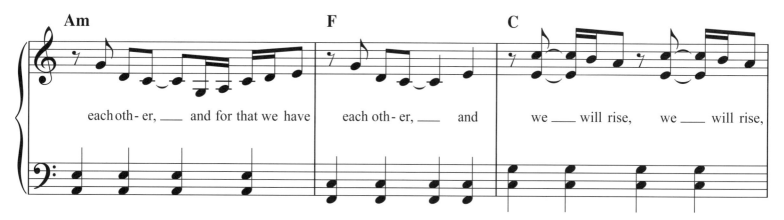

_____ up high _ like the waves. _ We'll rise _____ up in spite _ of the ache. _ We'll rise _

_____ up and we'll do it a thou - sand _____ times a - gain _____ for

you, _____ for you, _____ you, _____ for

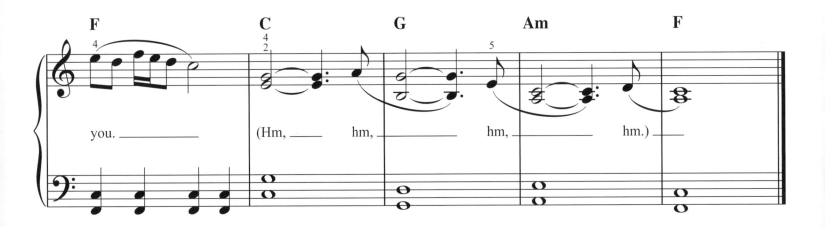

you. _____ (Hm, ____ hm, _____ hm, _____ hm.) ____

SCARS TO YOUR BEAUTIFUL

Words and Music by ALESSIA CARACCIOLO,
WARREN FELDER, COLERIDGE TILLMAN
and ANDREW WANSEL

Moderate Pop beat

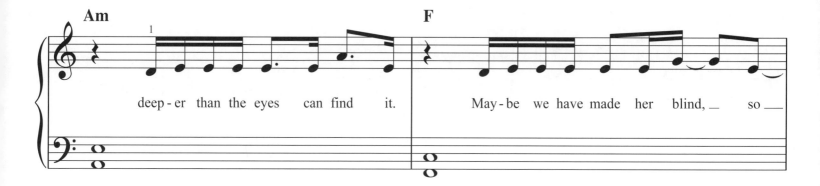

she tries to cov-er up ___ her pain ___ and cut her woes ___ a - way. ___

'Cause cov-er girls ___ don't cry ___ af-ter their face ___ is made. ___ But ___ there's a

hope that's wait-ing for you ___ in the dark. You should know you're beau-ti-ful just the way you

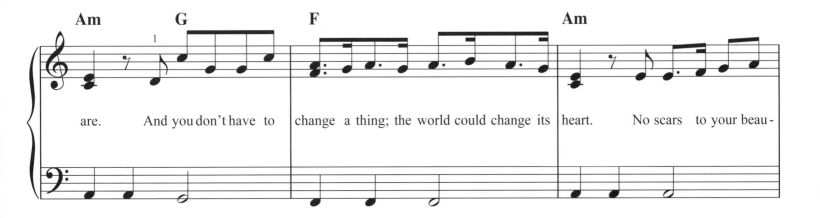

are. And you don't have to change a thing; the world could change its heart. No scars to your beau-

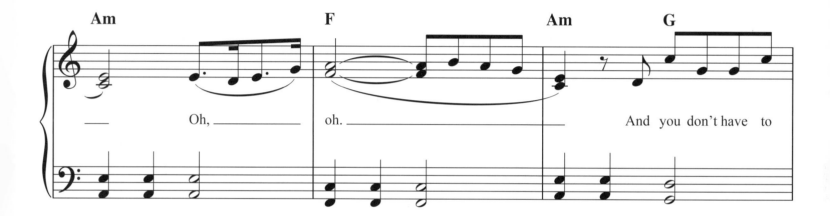

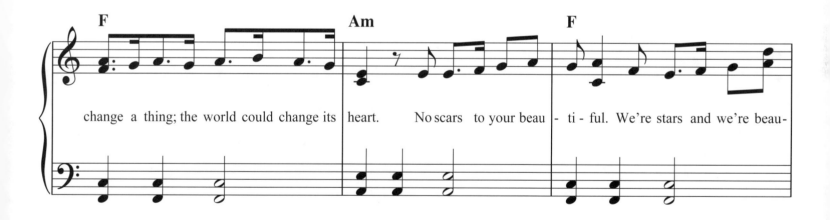

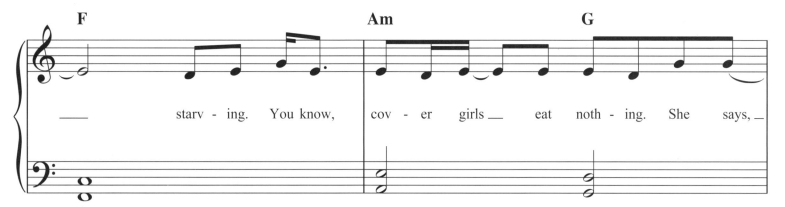

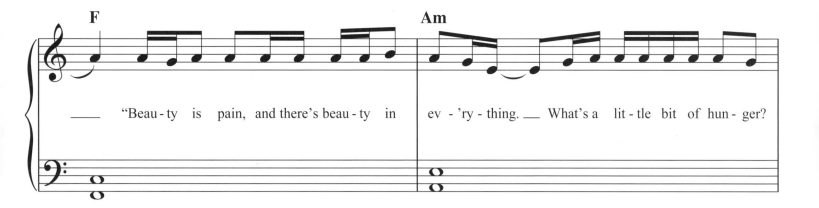

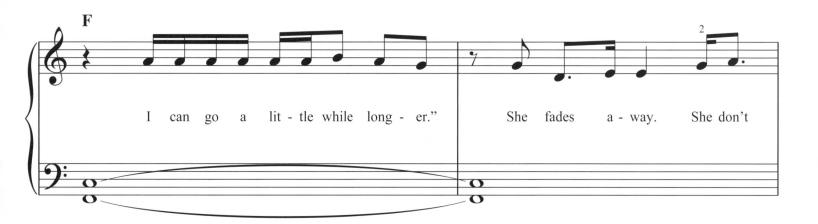

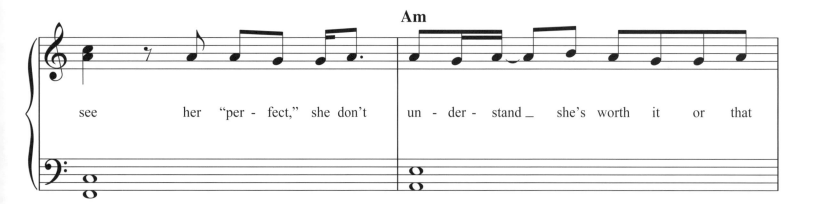

beau - ty goes deep - er than the sur - face, oh, _____ oh. _____ So, to all _____

_____ the girls _____ that's hurt - ing, let me be your mir - ror, help you see a

lit - tle bit clear - er the light that shines _____ with - in. _____ There's a

D.S. al Coda

CODA

N.C.

No bet - ter you than the you that you are. (No bet - ter you than the you that you are.)

No bet - ter life than the life we're liv - ing. (No bet - ter life than the life we're liv - ing.)

No bet - ter time for your shine; you're a star. (No bet - ter time for your shine.) Oh, you're beau -

ti - ful. ___ Oh, you're beau - ti - ful. ___ There's a hope that's wait - ing for you ___ in the

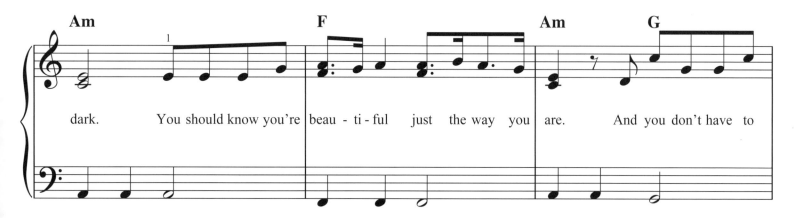

dark. You should know you're beau - ti - ful just the way you are. And you don't have to

change a thing; the world could change its heart. No scars to your beau - ti - ful. We're stars and we're beau -

ti - ful. _____ Oh, ___ oh. _____ Oh, _____

oh. _____ And you don't have to change a thing; the world could change its

heart. No scars to your beau - ti - ful. We're stars and we're beau - ti - ful. _____

STAY

Words and Music by ALESSIA CARACCIOLO,
ANDERS FROEN, JONNALI PARMENIUS,
SARAH AARONS, ANTON ZASLAVSKI
and LINUS WIKLUND

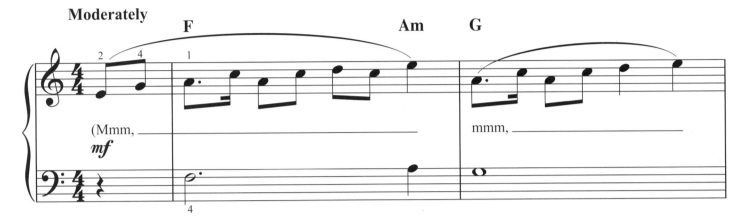

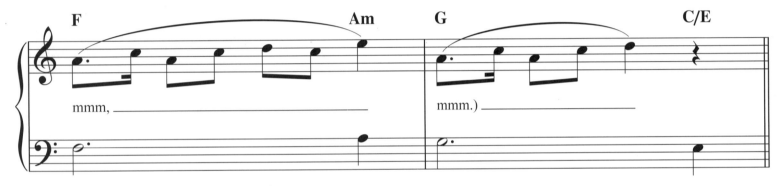

Wait- ing for the time to pass you by, _____
Won't ad- mit what I al- read- y know, _____ I've

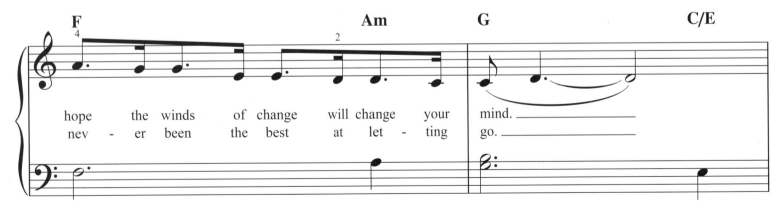

hope the winds of change will change your mind. _____
nev- er been the best at let- ting go.

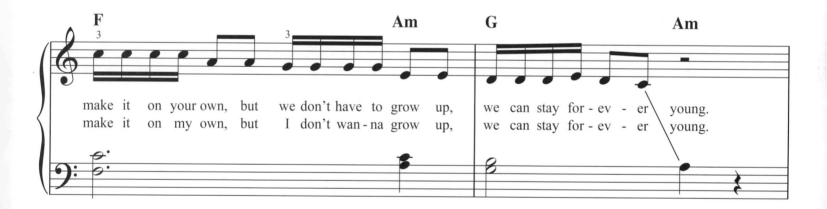

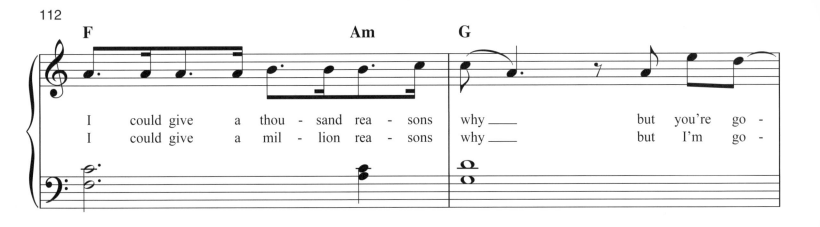

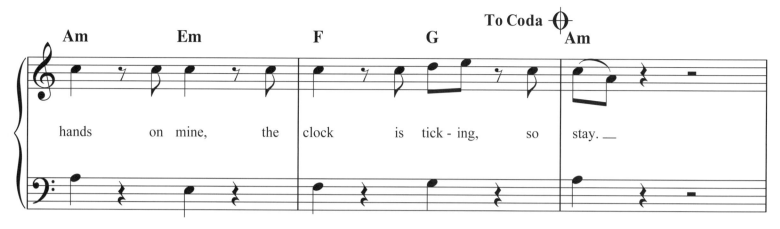

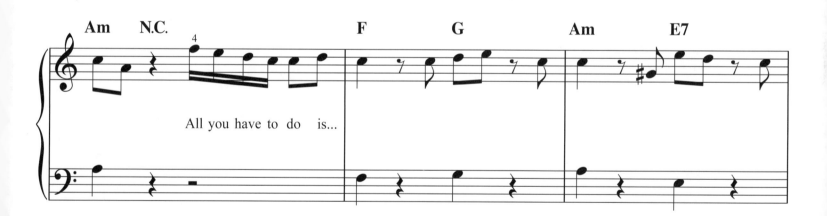

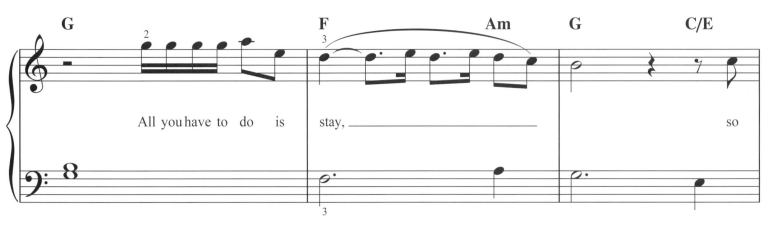

A THOUSAND MILES

Words and Music by
VANESSA CARLTON

Moderately fast

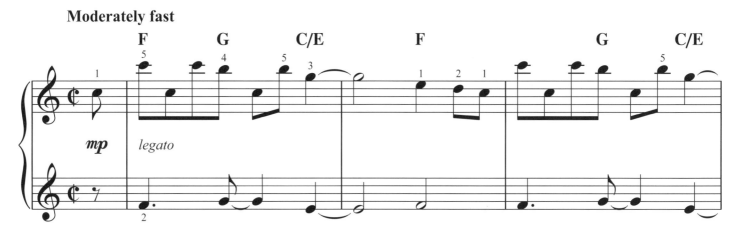

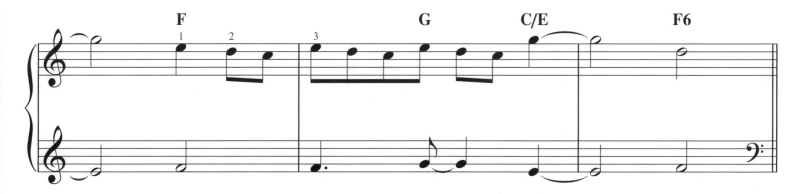

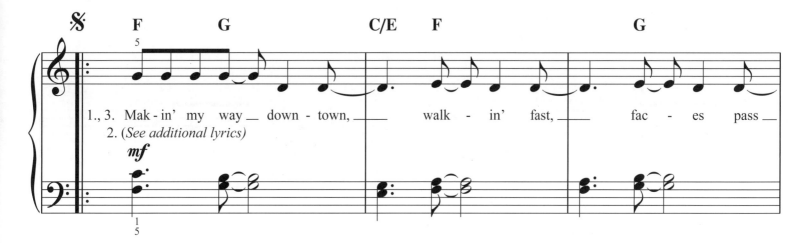

1., 3. Mak-in' my way __ down-town, __ walk-in' fast, __ fac-es pass __
2. (See additional lyrics)

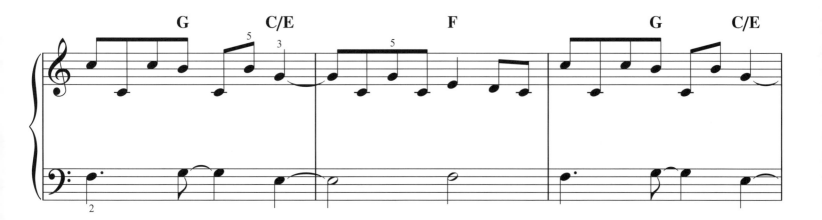

And I need you, ___

and I miss you,

and now I won - der... If I could _ fall _

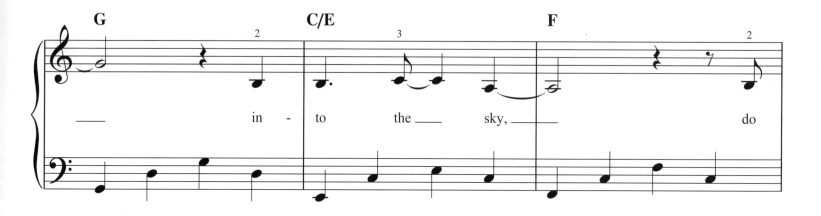

___ in - to the ___ sky, ___ do

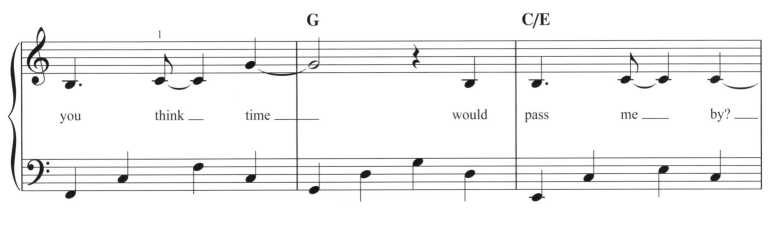

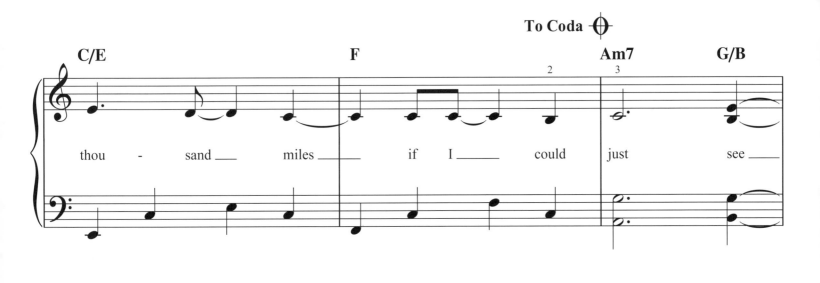

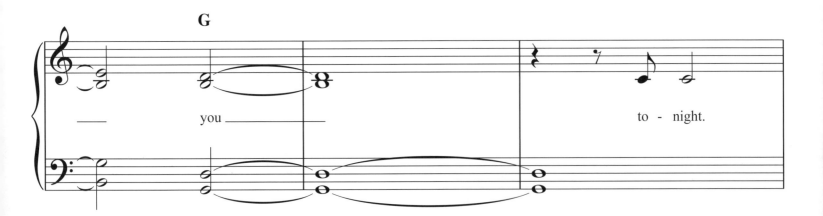

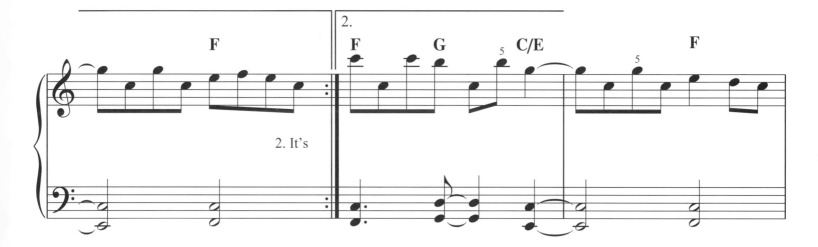

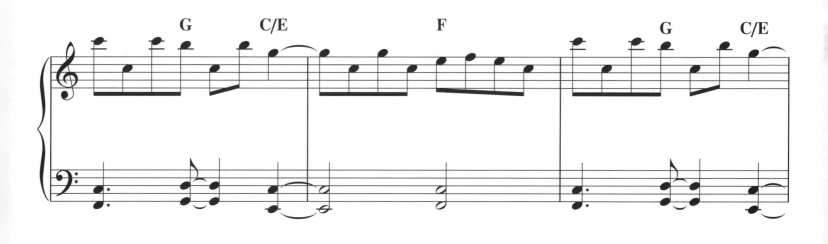

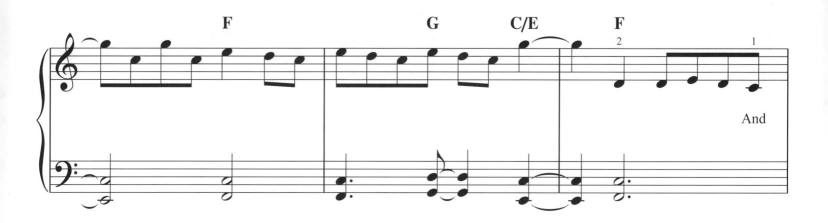

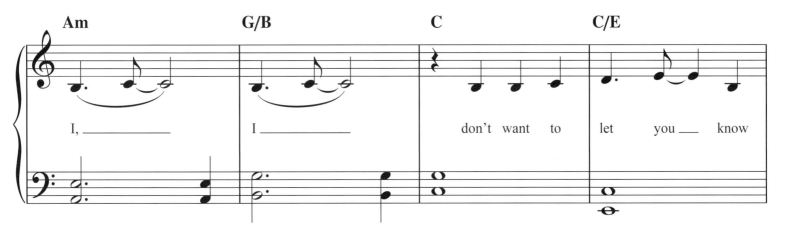

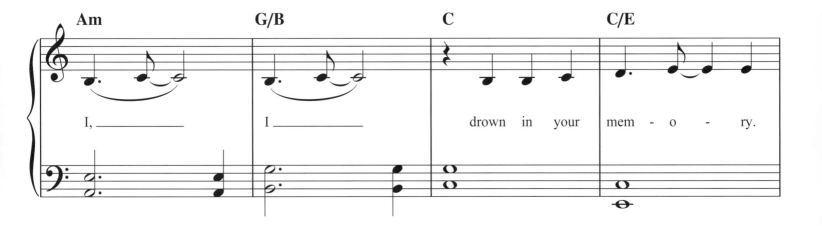

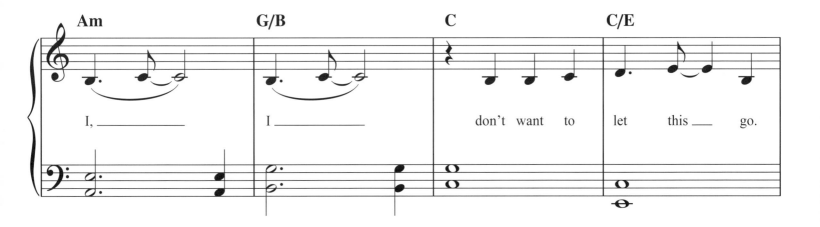

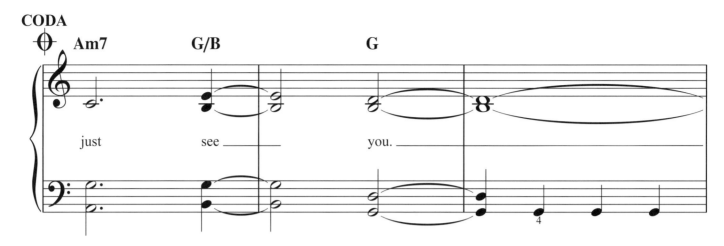

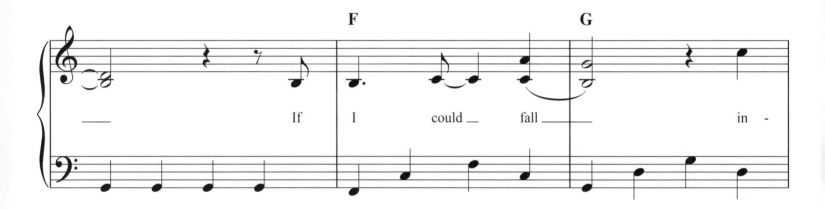

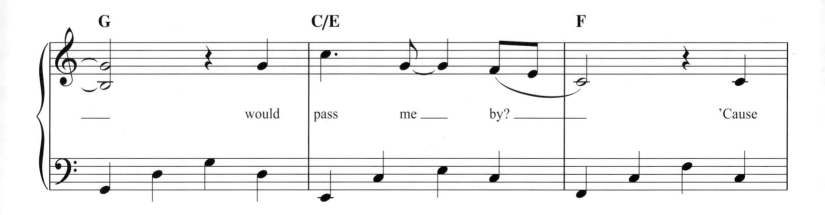

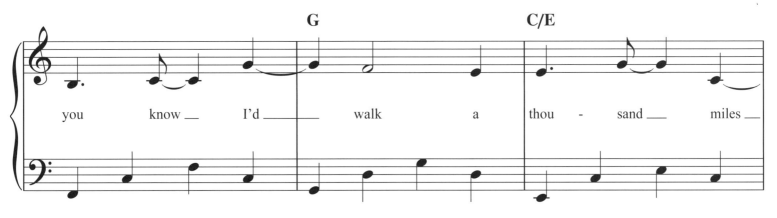

you know ___ I'd ___ walk a thou - sand ___ miles ___

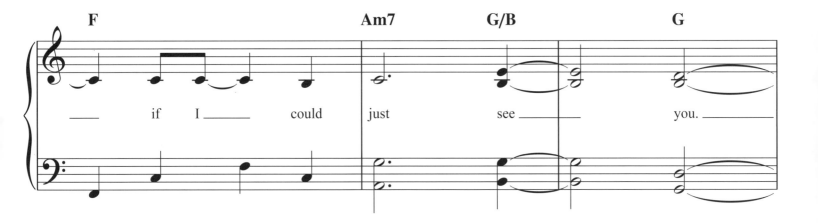

___ if I ___ could just see ___ you. ___

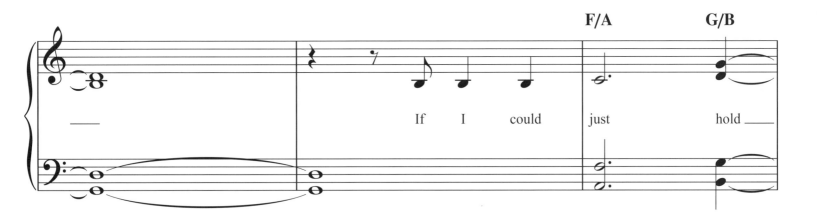

___ If I could just hold ___

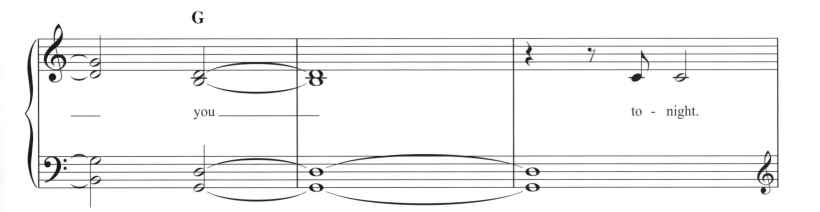

___ you ___ to - night.

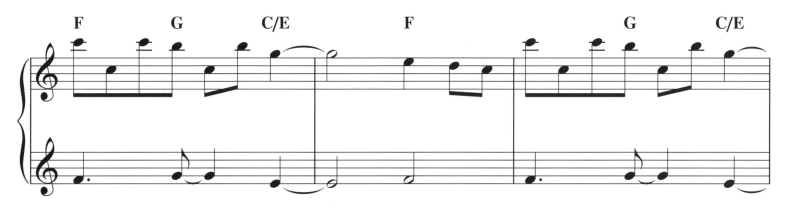

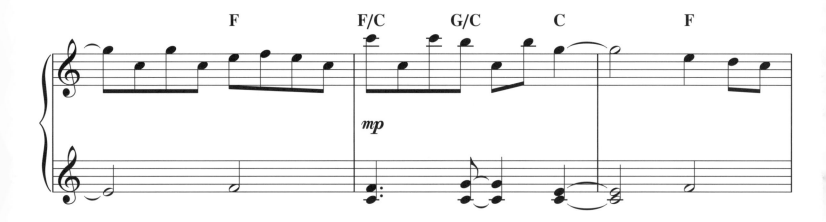

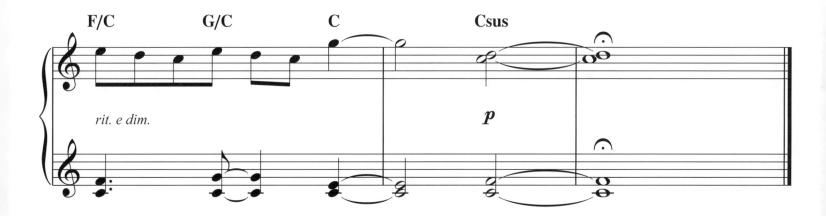

Additional Lyrics

2. It's always times like these when I think of you
   And wonder if you ever think of me.
   'Cause everything's so wrong and I don't belong
   Livin' in your precious memory.
   'Cause I need you,
   And I miss you,
   And I wonder....
   Chorus

THERE'S NOTHING HOLDIN' ME BACK

Words and Music by SHAWN MENDES,
GEOFFREY WARBURTON, TEDDY GEIGER
and SCOTT HARRIS

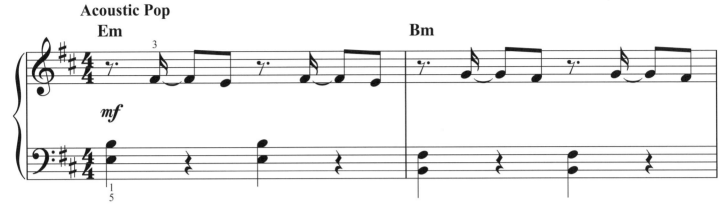

I want to fol-low where she goes,
She says that she's nev-er a-fraid;

I think a-bout her and she
just pic-ture ev-'ry-bod-y

knows it. ___
na-ked. ___

I want to let her take con-trol,
She real-ly does-n't like to wait,

'cause ev - 'ry time that she gets clos - er, she pulls me in e-
not real - ly in - to hes - i - ta - tion. Pulls

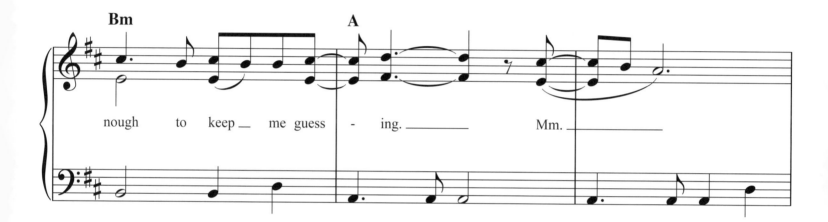

nough to keep me guess - ing. Mm.

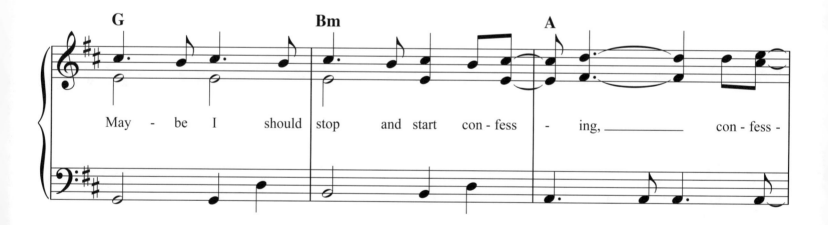

May - be I should stop and start con - fess - ing, con - fess-

- ing, yeah. Oh, I've been shak-ing, I love you when you go cra - zy. You take

all my in-hi-bi-tions, ba - by, there's noth-ing hold-in' me back. You take me plac-es that tear

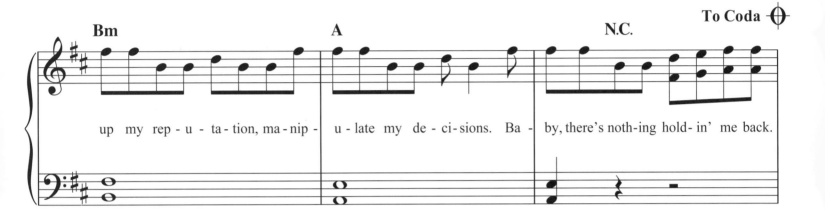

To Coda ⊕

up my rep-u-ta-tion, ma-nip - u-late my de-ci-sions. Ba - by, there's noth-ing hold-in' me back.

There's noth-ing hold-in' me back.

There's noth-ing hold-in' me back.   'Cause if we

lost our minds and we took __ it way too far, I know we'd be al - right, I know we __

__ would be al-right. If you were by my side and we stum - bled in the dark, I know we'd

be al - right, I know we __ would be al-right, 'Cause if we lost our minds and we took __

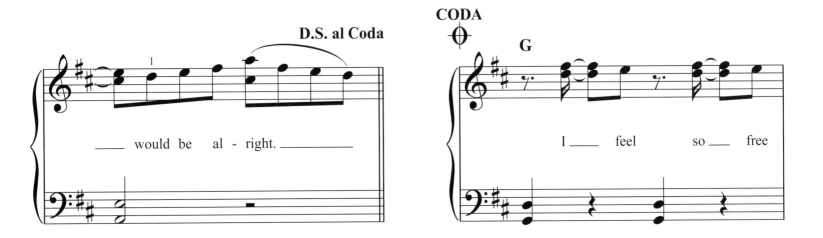

WHATEVER IT TAKES

Words and Music by DAN REYNOLDS,
WAYNE SERMON, BEN McKEE,
DANIEL PLATZMAN and JOEL LITTLE

Half-time Pop beat

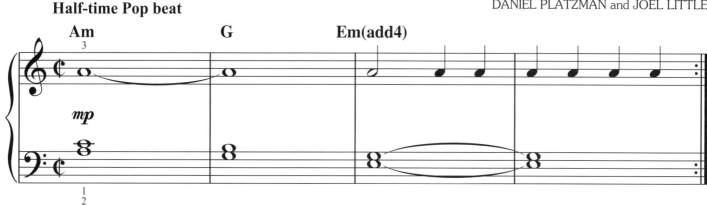

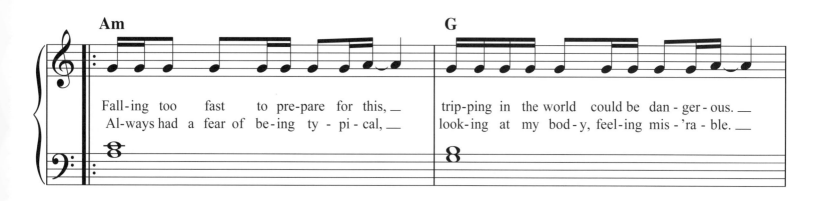

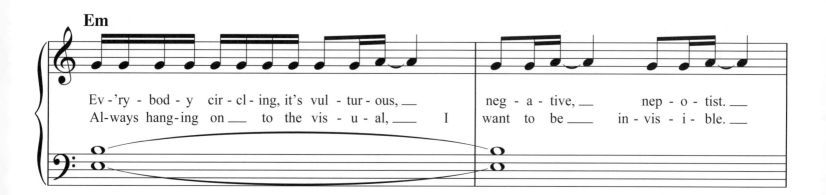

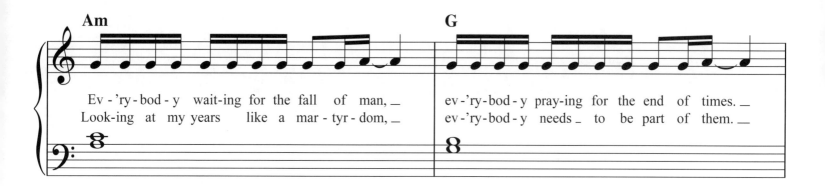

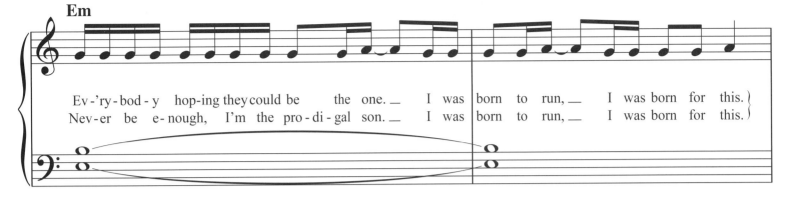

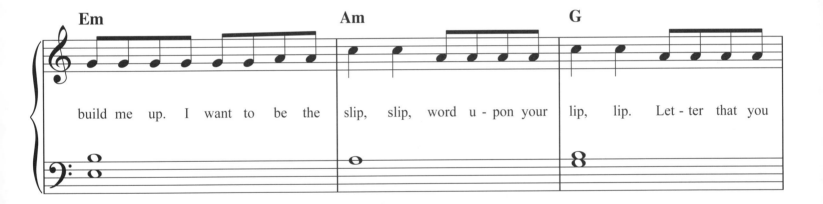

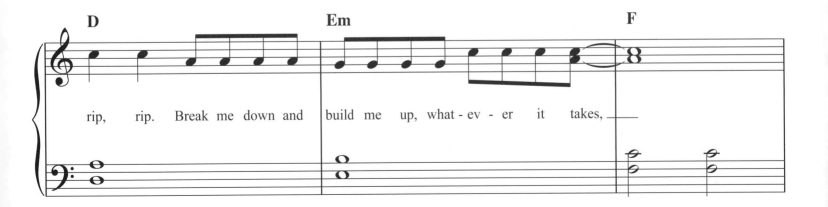

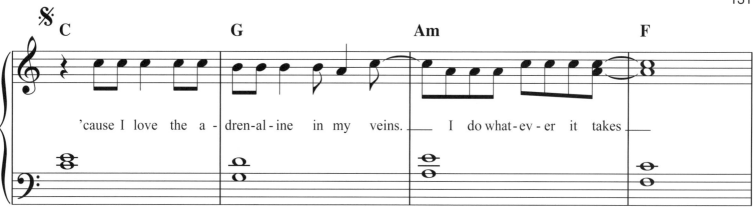

'cause I love the a - dren-al-ine in my veins.___ I do what-ev-er it takes

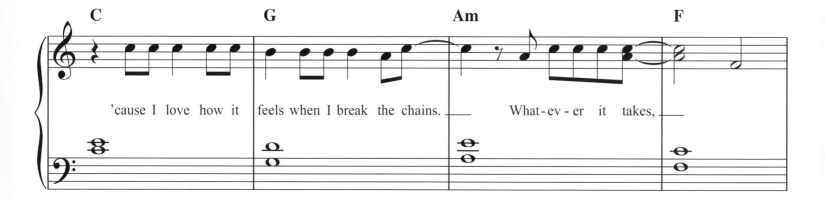

'cause I love how it feels when I break the chains.___ What-ev-er it takes,

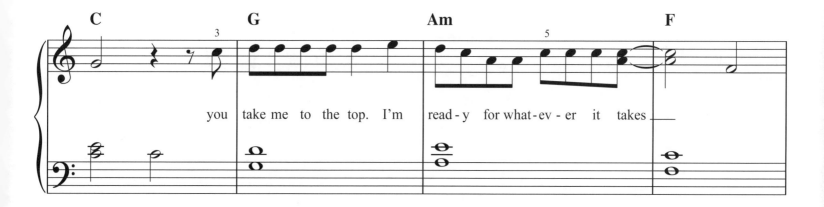

you take me to the top. I'm read-y for what-ev-er it takes

To Coda

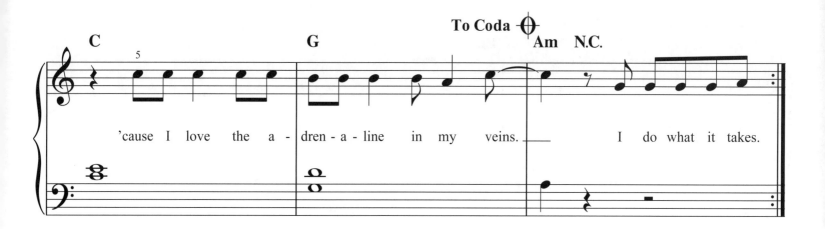

'cause I love the a - dren-a-line in my veins.___ I do what it takes.

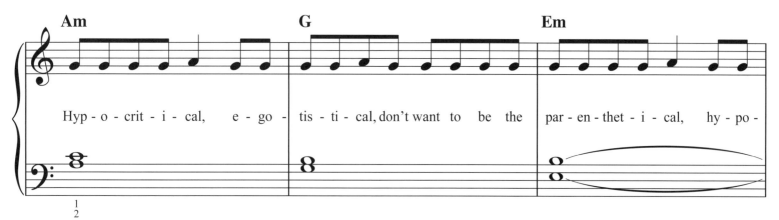

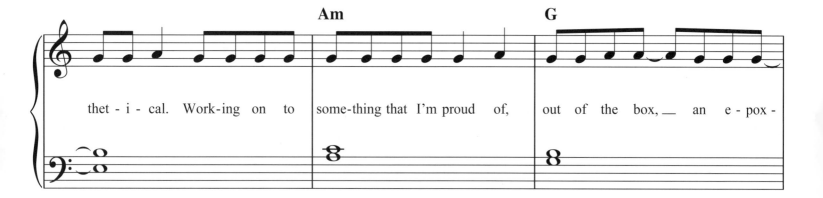

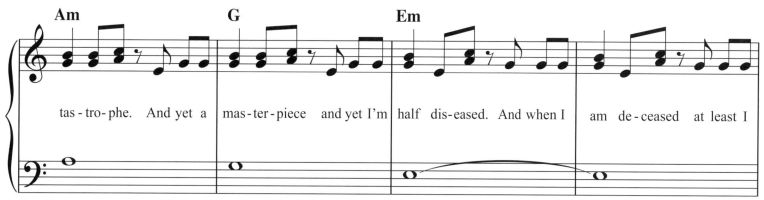

tas-tro-phe. And yet a mas-ter-piece and yet I'm half dis-eased. And when I am de-ceased at least I

go down to the grave and die hap-pi-ly. Leave the bod-y of my soul to be a

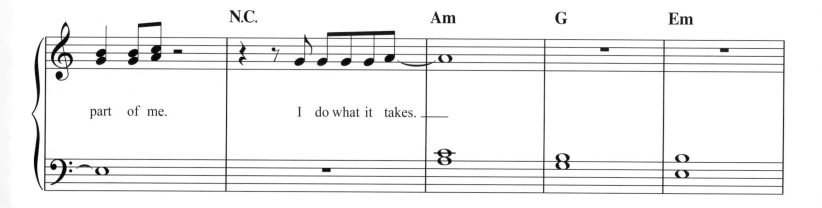

part of me. I do what it takes.

What-ev-er it takes

I do what it takes.

TOO GOOD AT GOODBYES

Words and Music by SAM SMITH,
TOR HERMANSEN, MIKKEL ERIKSEN
and JAMES NAPIER

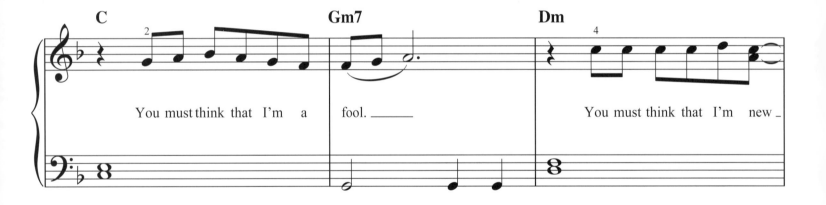

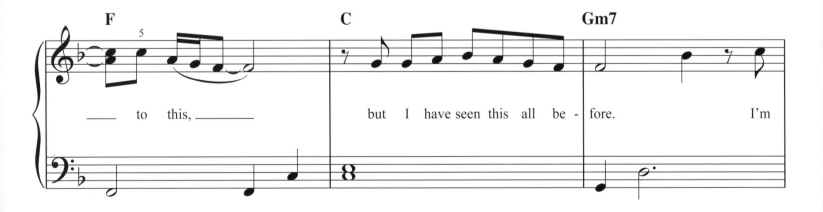

never gon-na let you close to me, e-ven though you mean the most to me. 'Cause

ev-'ry time I o-pen up, it hurts. _____ So I'm

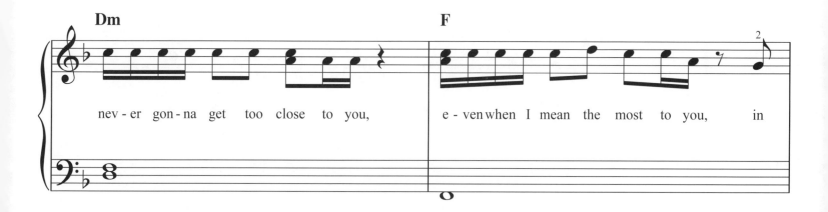

nev-er gon-na get too close to you, e-ven when I mean the most to you, in

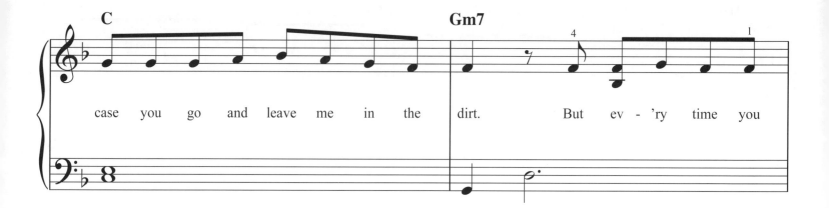

case you go and leave me in the dirt. But ev-'ry time you

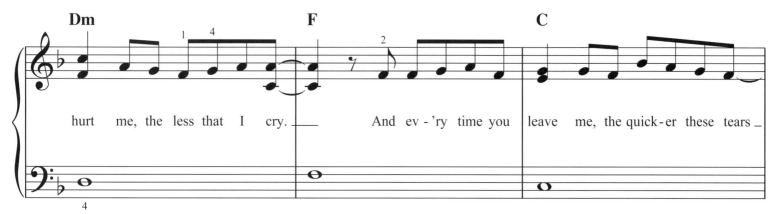

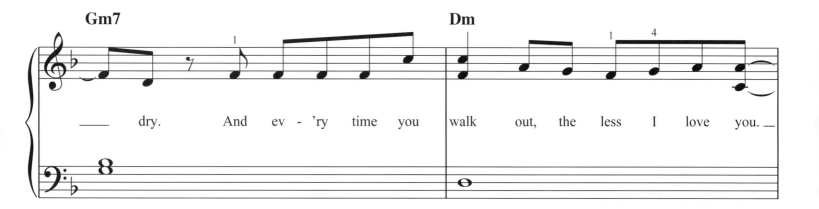

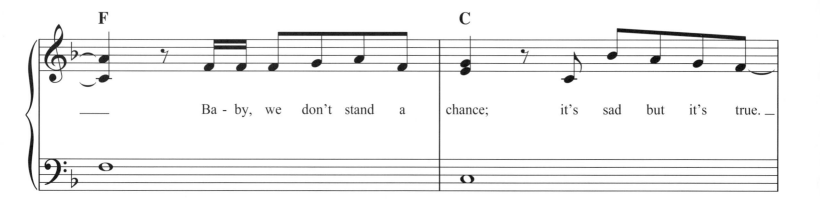

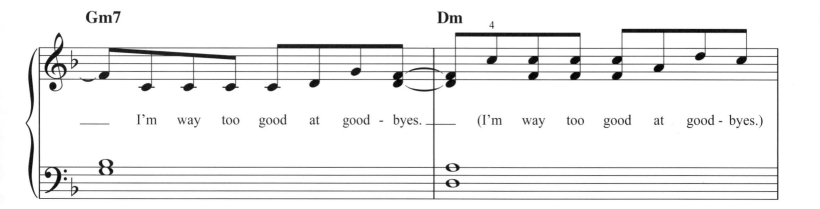

I'm way too good at good-byes.　　(I'm way too good at good-byes.)

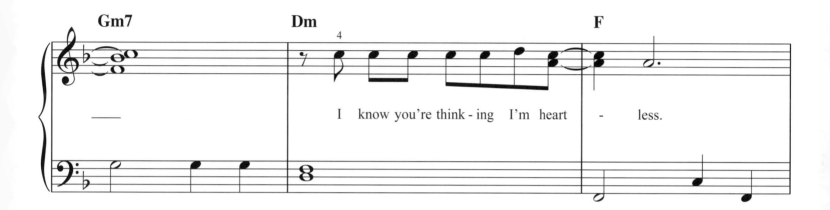

I know you're think-ing I'm heart-less.

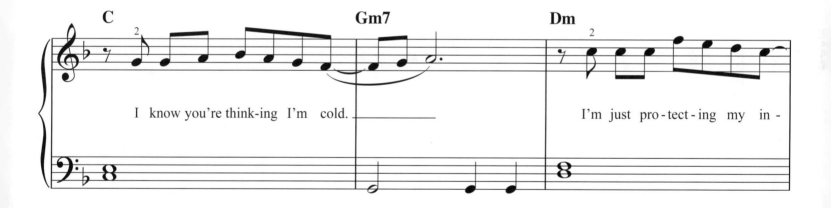

I know you're think-ing I'm cold.　　I'm just pro-tect-ing my in-

-no-cence.　　I'm just pro-tect-ing my soul.　　I'm

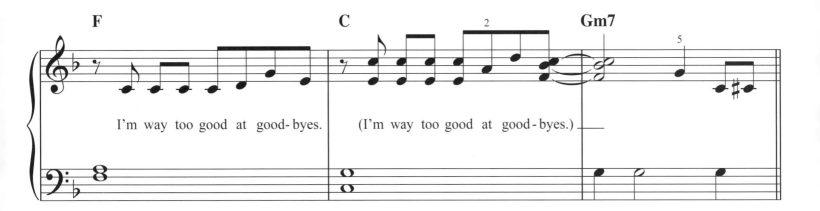

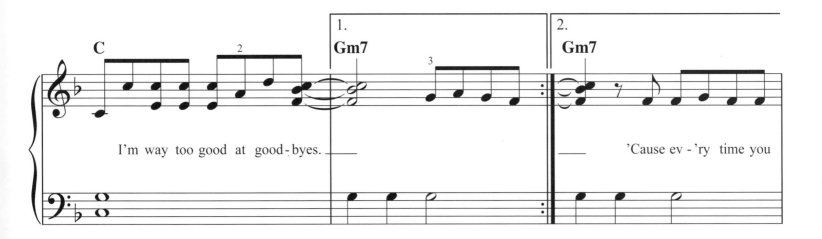

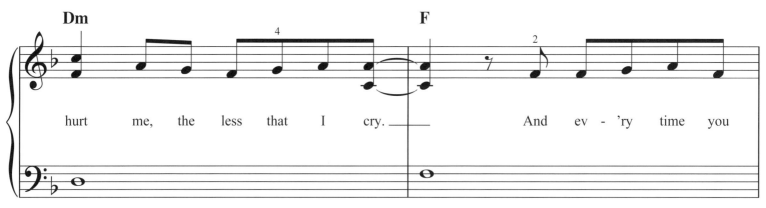

hurt me, the less that I cry._____ And ev - 'ry time you

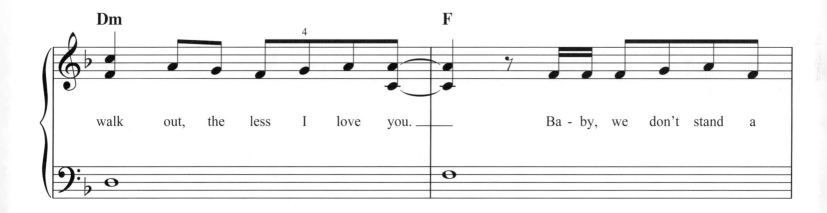

leave me, the quick - er these tears_____ dry. And ev - 'ry time you

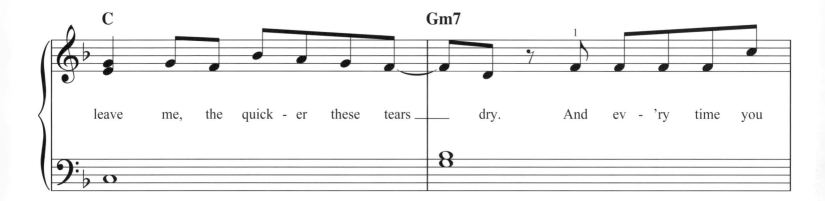

walk out, the less I love you._____ Ba - by, we don't stand a

chance; it's sad but it's true._____ I'm way too good at good - byes._____

WHAT ABOUT US

Words and Music by ALECIA MOORE,
STEVE MAC and JOHNNY McDAID

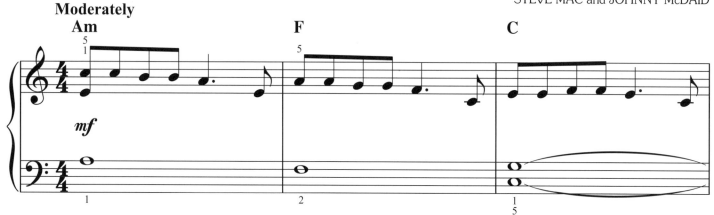

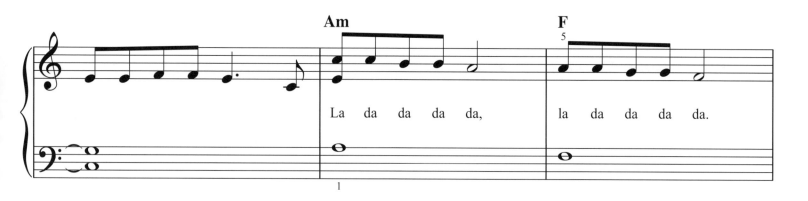

La da da da da, la da da da da.

Da da da da da. We are search-
prob-

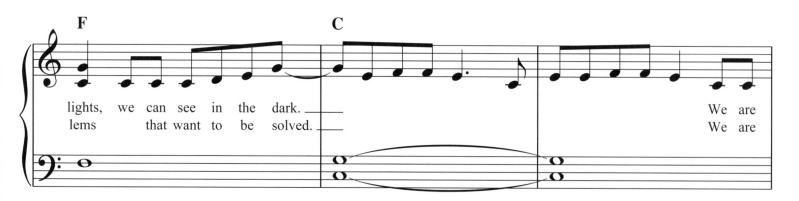

lights, we can see in the dark. We are
lems that want to be solved. We are

rock - ets, point-ed up at the stars. ___
chil - dren that need to be loved. ___

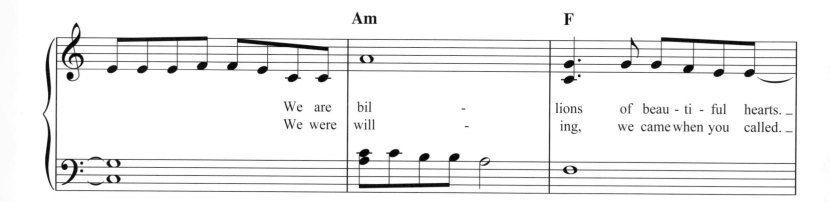

We are bil - lions of beau - ti - ful hearts. ___
We were will - ing, we came when you called. ___

And you sold
But you fooled

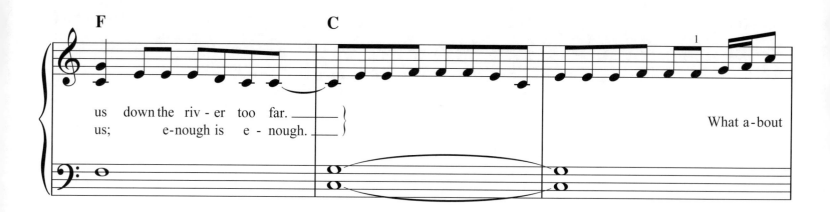

us down the riv - er too far. ___
us; e-nough is e - nough. ___

What a-bout

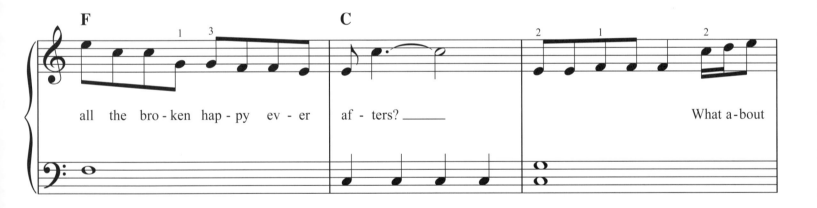

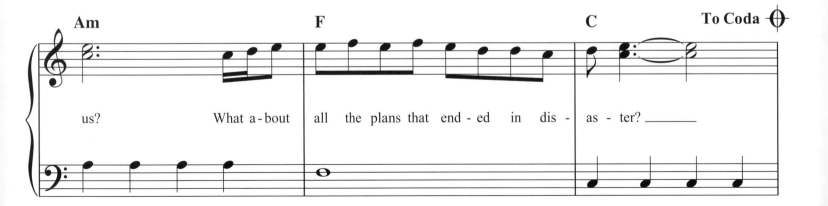

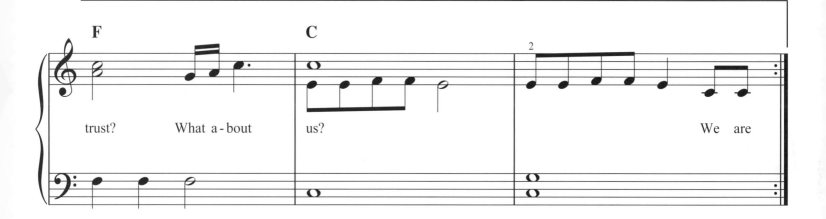

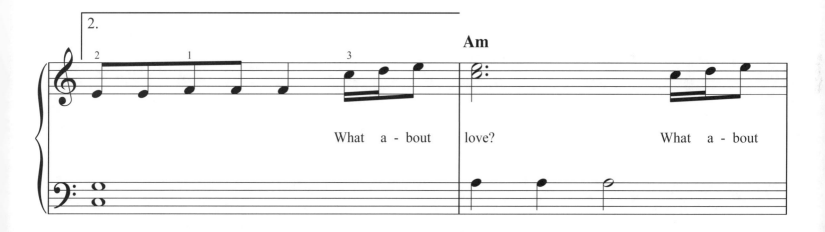

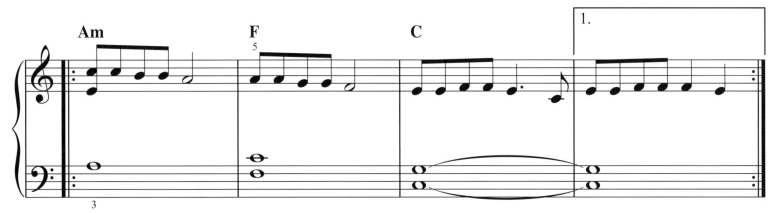

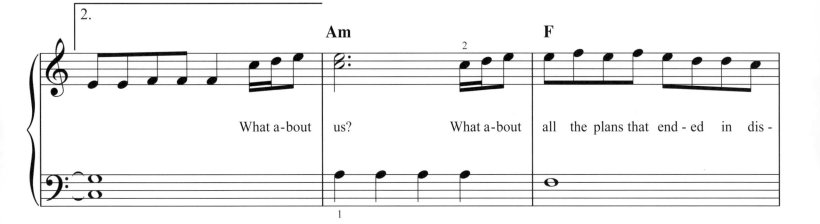

What a-bout us? What a-bout all the plans that end-ed in dis-

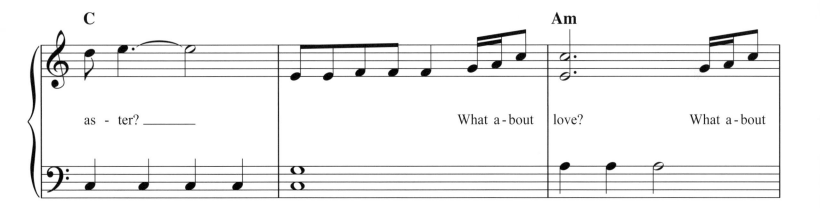

as - ter? _____ What a-bout love? What a-bout

trust? What a-bout us?

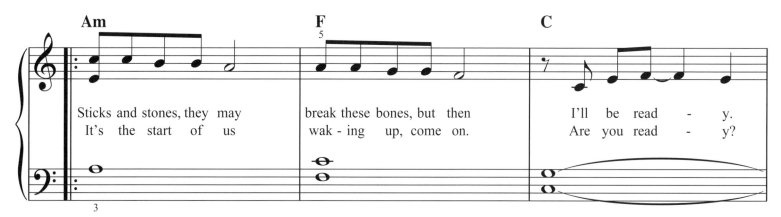

Sticks and stones, they may
It's the start of us

break these bones, but then
wak - ing up, come on.

I'll be read - y.
Are you read - y?

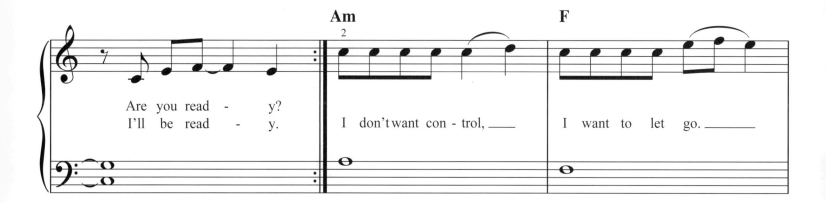

Are you read - y?
I'll be read - y.

I don't want con - trol, _____

I want to let go. _____

Are you read - y?

I'll be read - y.

Now it's time to

D.S. al Coda

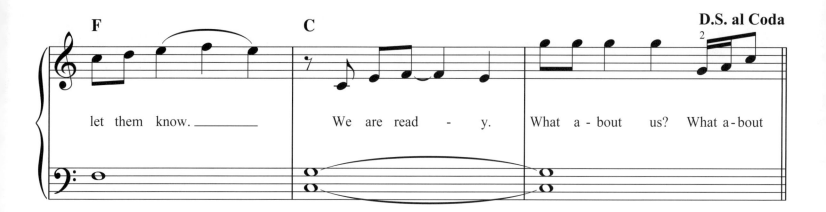

let them know. _____

We are read - y.

What a - bout us? What a - bout

CODA

Oh, what a-bout love? What a-bout trust? What a-bout

us? What a-bout us? What a-bout

us? What a-bout _____ us? What a-bout

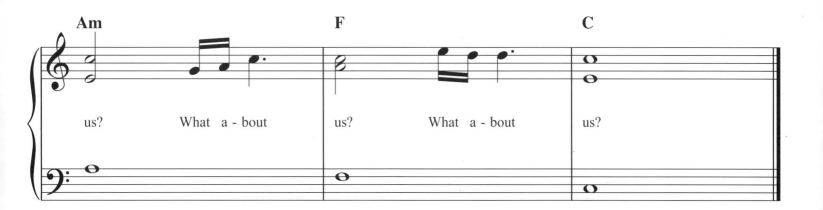

us? What a-bout us? What a-bout us?

YOU WILL BE FOUND

from DEAR EVAN HANSEN

Music and Lyrics by BENJ PASEK
and JUSTIN PAUL

Reverent, quasi rubato

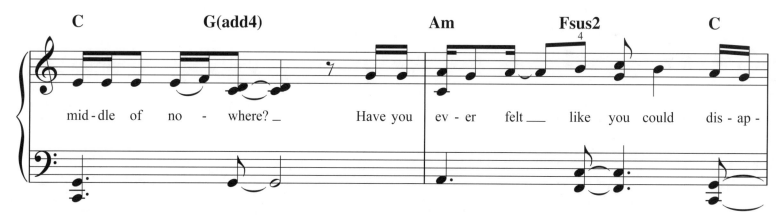

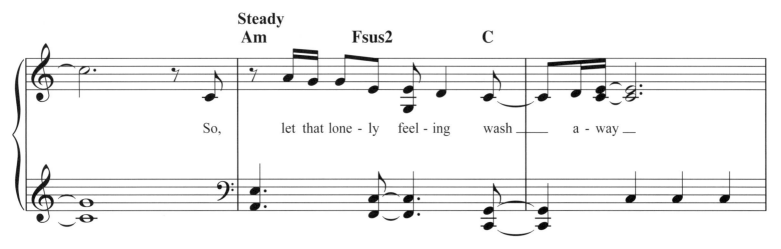

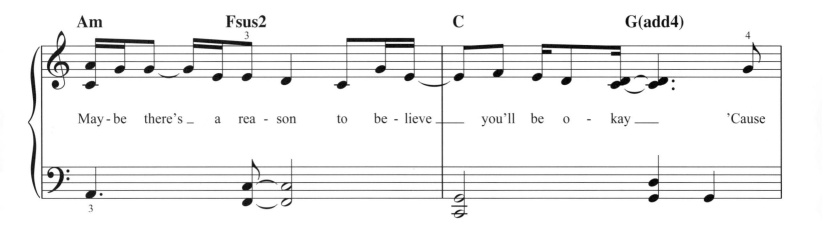

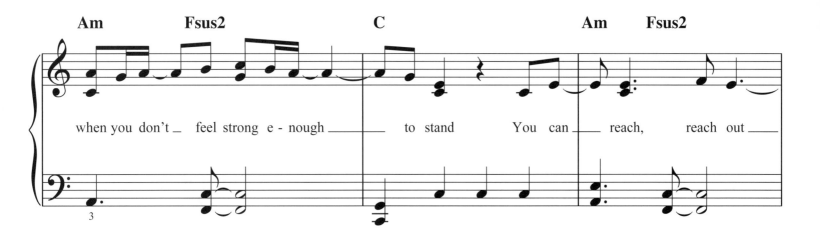

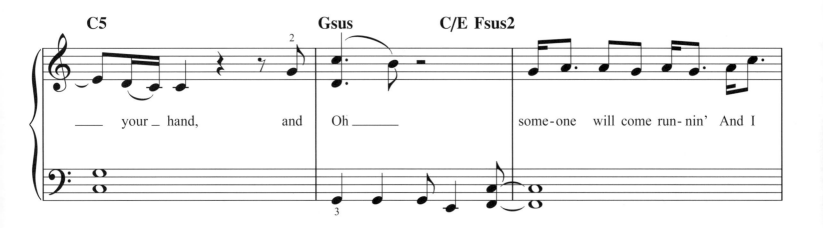

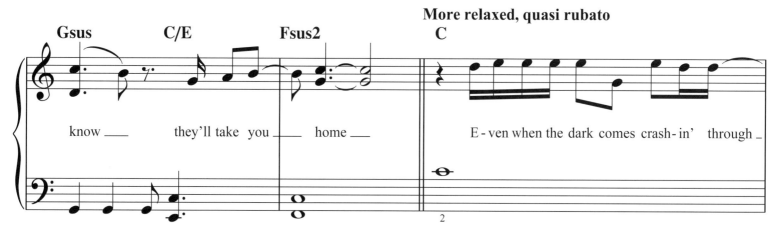

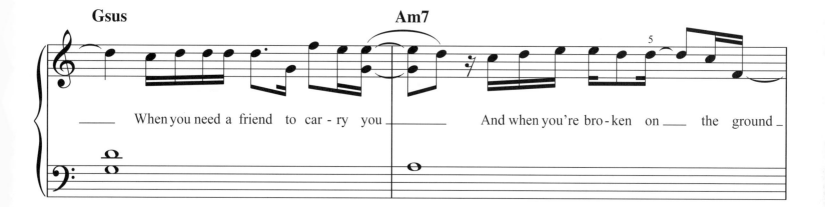

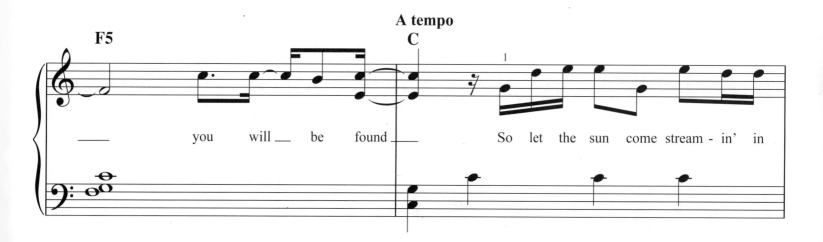

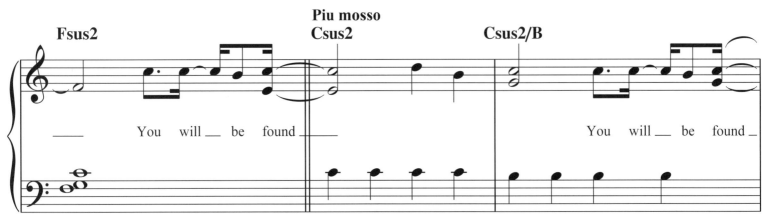

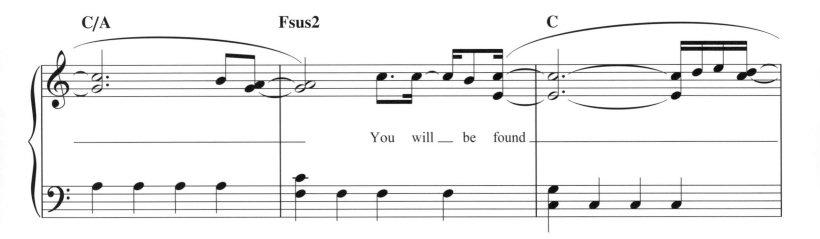

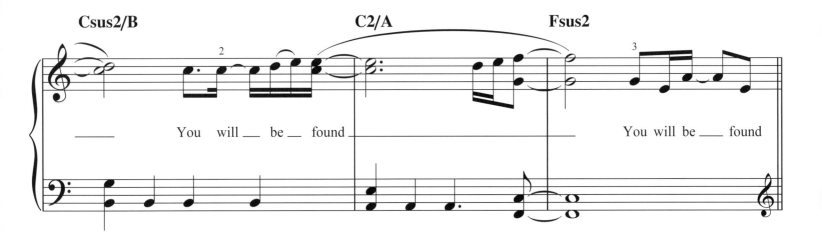

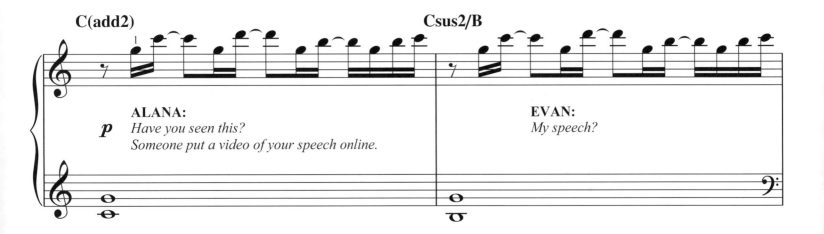

Csus/A ... **F(add2)**

ALANA: *People started sharing it, I guess and now, I mean Connor is everywhere.*

JARED: *Your speech is everywhere.*

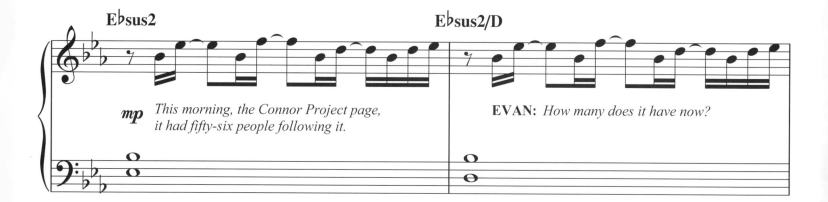

E♭sus2 ... **E♭sus2/D**

mp *This morning, the Connor Project page, it had fifty-six people following it.*

EVAN: *How many does it have now?*

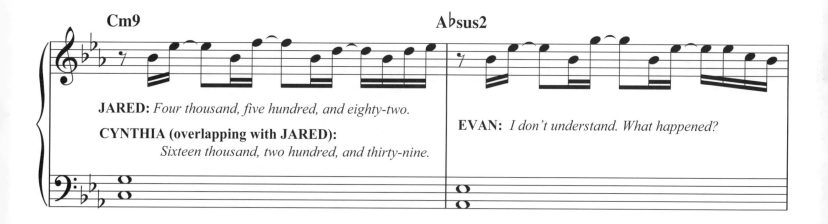

Cm9 ... **A♭sus2**

JARED: *Four thousand, five hundred, and eighty-two.*

CYNTHIA (overlapping with JARED): *Sixteen thousand, two hundred, and thirty-nine.*

EVAN: *I don't understand. What happened?*

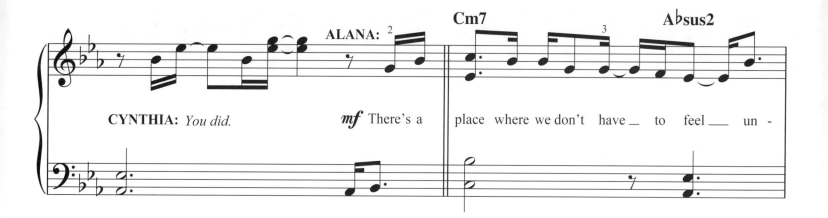

Cm7 ... **A♭sus2**

ALANA:

CYNTHIA: *You did.*

mf There's a place where we don't have __ to feel __ un-

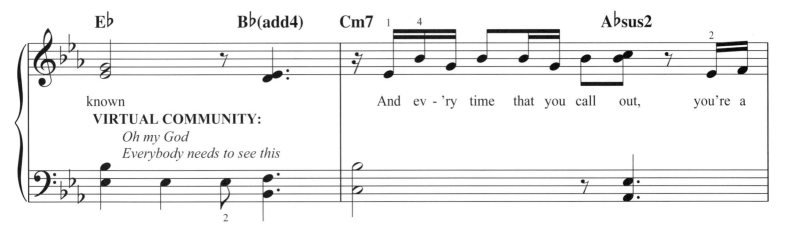

known

VIRTUAL COMMUNITY:
Oh my God
Everybody needs to see this

And ev-'ry time that you call out, you're a

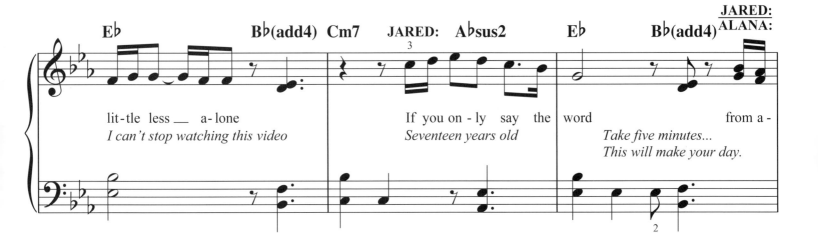

lit-tle less __ a-lone
I can't stop watching this video

JARED:
If you on-ly say the word
Seventeen years old

JARED:
ALANA:
from a-
Take five minutes...
This will make your day.

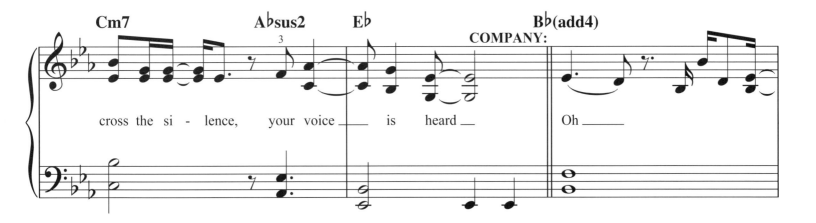

cross the si - lence, your voice __ is heard __

COMPANY:
Oh __

Share it with the people you love
Re-Post
The world needs to hear this
A beautiful tribute
Favorite

Oh __

I know someone who really needed to hear this today.
So thank you, Evan Hansen, for doing what you're doing.

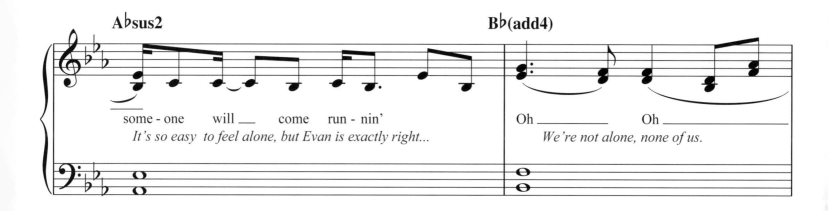

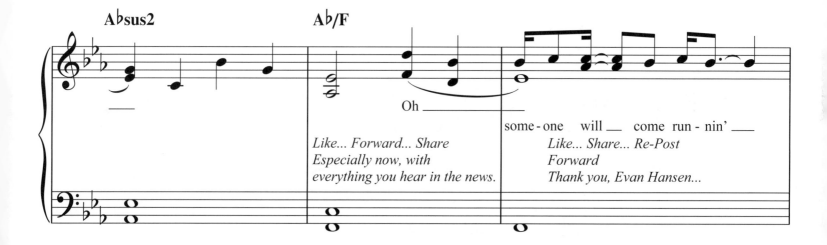

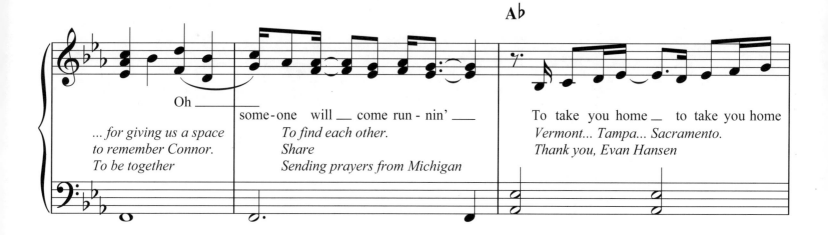

Some-one will __ come run-nin' to take you home __ To take you home __ To take you home __
Re-Post... Watch until the end
Thank you, Evan Hansen
This video is everything right now
All the feels... Thank you, thank you

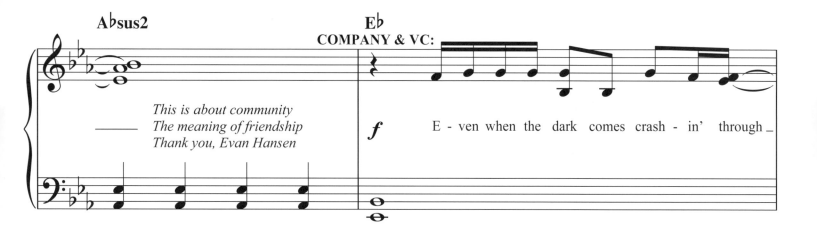

A♭sus2

E♭
COMPANY & VC:

This is about community
The meaning of friendship
Thank you, Evan Hansen

f E - ven when the dark comes crash - in' through __

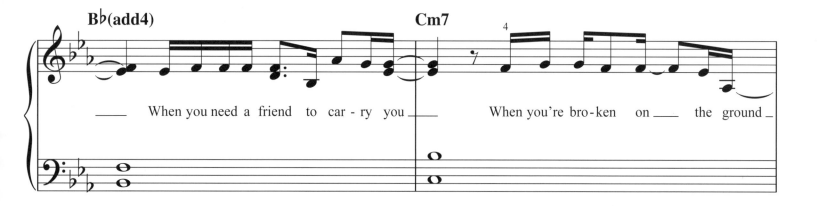

B♭(add4)

Cm7

__ When you need a friend to car - ry you __ When you're bro-ken on __ the ground __

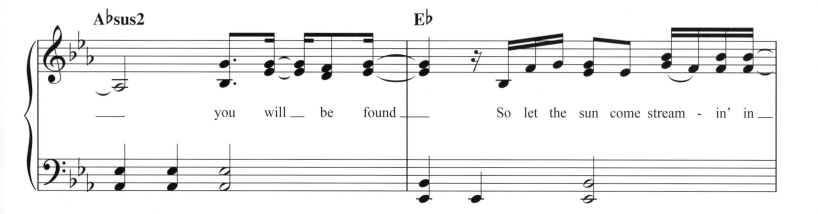

A♭sus2

E♭

__ you will __ be found __ So let the sun come stream - in' in __

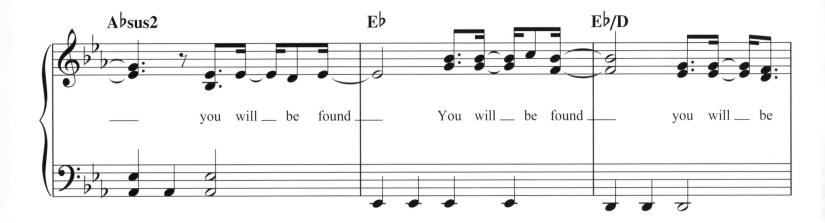

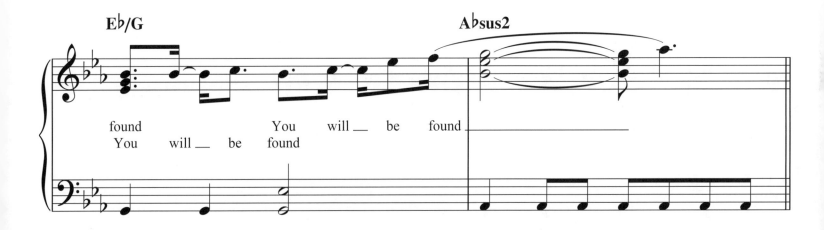

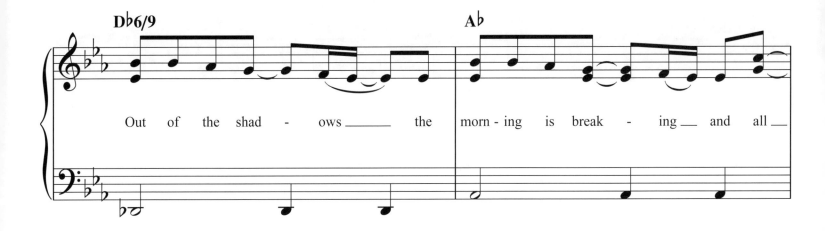

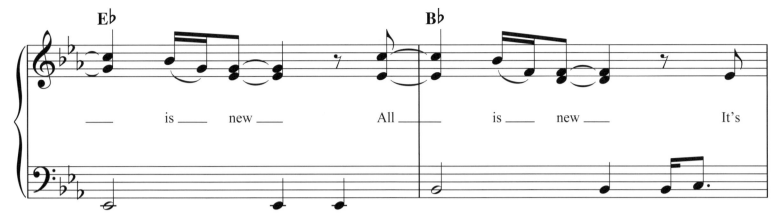

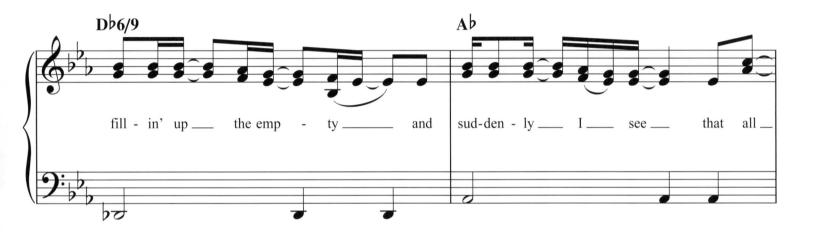

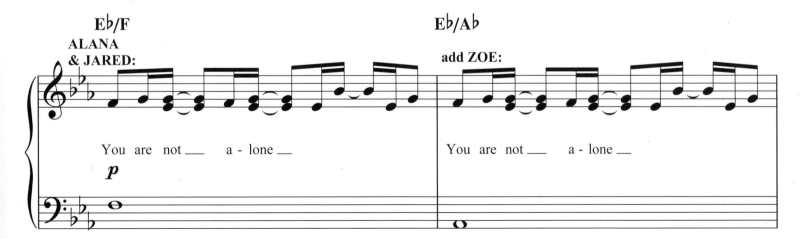

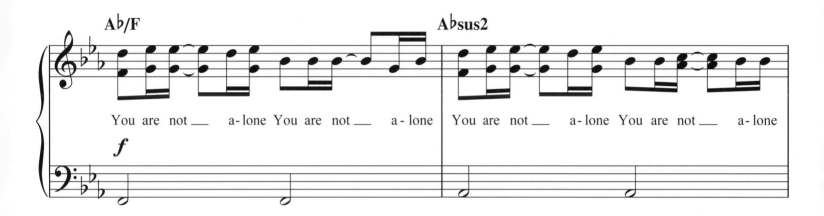

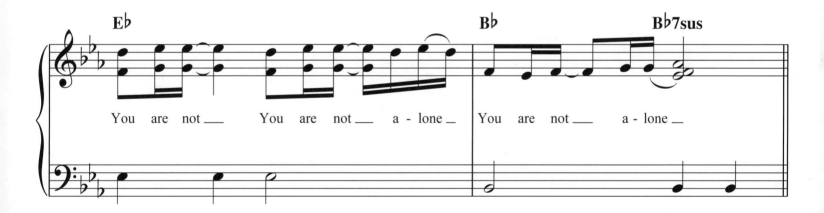

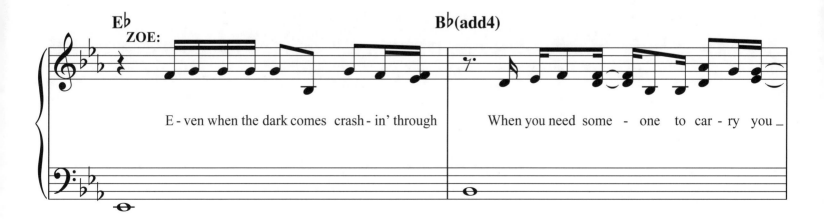

Cm7

When you're bro - ken on ____ the ground ____

A♭sus2

ALANA/CYNTHIA
HEIDI/JARED/LARRY:

You will ____ be found ____

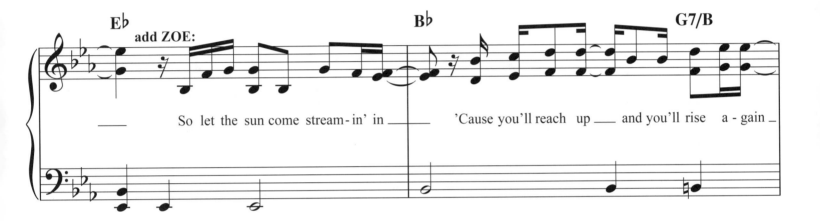

E♭

add ZOE:

So let the sun come stream - in' in ____

B♭

'Cause you'll reach up ____ and you'll rise a - gain ____

G7/B

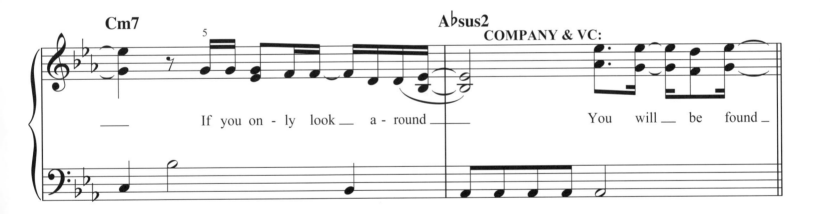

Cm7

If you on - ly look ____ a - round ____

A♭sus2

COMPANY & VC:

You will ____ be found ____

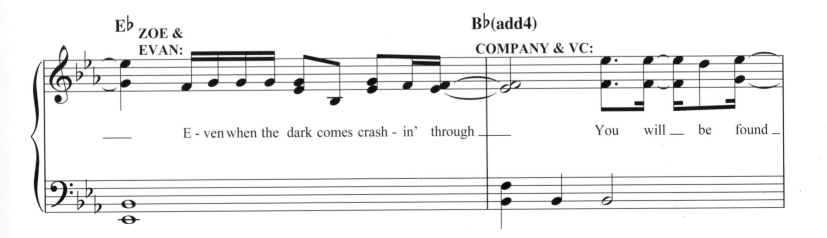

E♭

ZOE &
EVAN:

E - ven when the dark comes crash - in' through ____

B♭(add4)

COMPANY & VC:

You will ____ be found ____

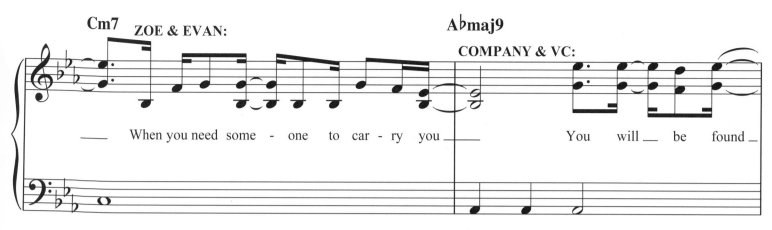

When you need some - one to car - ry you You will __ be found __

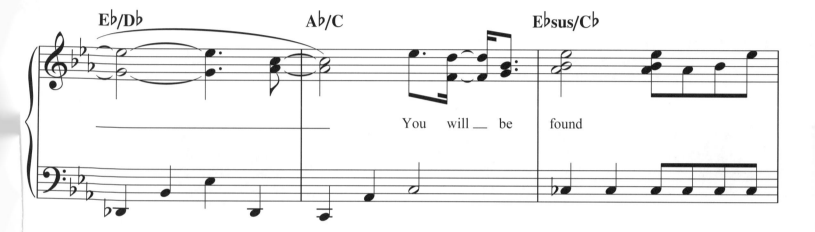

You will __ be found

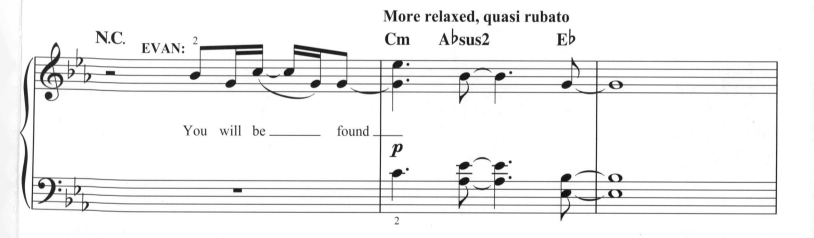

You will be _____ found __

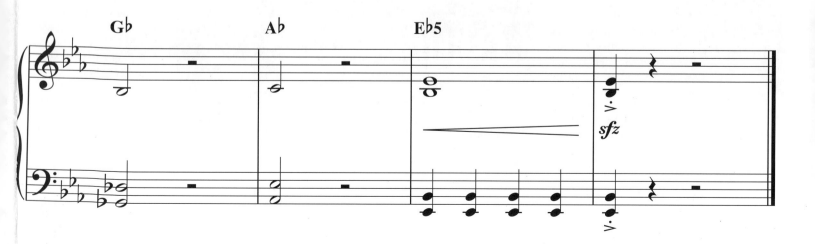

It's Easy to Play Your Favorite Songs with Hal Leonard Easy Piano Books

The Best Praise & Worship Songs Ever

The name says it all: over 70 of the best P&W songs today. Titles include: Awesome God • Blessed Be Your Name • Come, Now Is the Time to Worship • Days of Elijah • Here I Am to Worship • Open the Eyes of My Heart • Shout to the Lord • We Fall Down • and more.
00311312 .... $19.99

First 50 Popular Songs You Should Play on the Piano

50 great pop classics for beginning pianists to learn, including: Candle in the Wind • Chopsticks • Don't Know Why • Hallelujah • Happy Birthday to You • Heart and Soul • I Walk the Line • Just the Way You Are • Let It Be • Let It Go • Over the Rainbow • Piano Man • and many more.
00131140 .... $16.99

The Greatest Video Game Music

28 easy piano selections for the music that envelops you as you lose yourself in the world of video games, including: Angry Birds Theme • Assassin's Creed Revelations • Dragonborn (Skyrim Theme) • Elder Scrolls: Oblivion • Minecraft: Sweden • Rage of Sparta from God of War III • and more.
00202545 .... $17.99

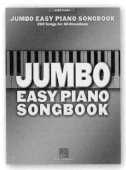

Jumbo Easy Piano Songbook

200 classical favorites, folk songs and jazz standards. Includes: Amazing Grace • Beale Street Blues • Bridal Chorus • Buffalo Gals • Canon in D • Cielito Lindo • Danny Boy • The Entertainer • Für Elise • Greensleeves • Jamaica Farewell • Marianne • Molly Malone • Ode to Joy • Peg O' My Heart • Rockin' Robin • Yankee Doodle • dozens more!
00311014 .... $19.99

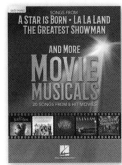

Songs from *A Star Is Born, The Greatest Showman, La La Land*, and More Movie Musicals

Movie musical lovers will delight in this songbook chock full of top-notch songs arranged for easy piano with lyrics from blockbuster movies. Includes: City of Stars from *La La Land* • Suddenly from *Les Misérables* • This Is Me from *The Greatest Showman* • Shallow from *A Star Is Born* • and more.
00287577 .... $17.99

50 Easy Classical Themes

Easy arrangements of 50 classical tunes representing more than 30 composers, including: Bach, Beethoven, Chopin, Debussy, Dvorak, Handel, Haydn, Liszt, Mozart, Mussorgsky, Puccini, Rossini, Schubert, Strauss, Tchaikovsky, Vivaldi, and more.
00311215 .... $14.99

Pop Songs for Kids

Kids from all corners of the world love and sing along to the songs of Taylor Swift, One Direction, Katy Perry, and other pop stars. This collection features 25 songs from these and many more artists in easy piano format. Includes: Brave • Can't Stop the Feeling • Firework • Home • Let It Go • Shake It Off • What Makes You Beautiful • and more.
00221920 .... $14.99

Simple Songs – The Easiest Easy Piano Songs

Play 50 of your favorite songs in the easiest of arrangements! Songs include: Castle on a Cloud • Do-Re-Mi • Happy Birthday to You • Hey Jude • Let It Go • Linus and Lucy • Over the Rainbow • Smile • Star Wars (Main Theme) • Tomorrow • and more.
00142041 .... $14.99

VH1's 100 Greatest Songs of Rock and Roll

The results from the VH1 show that featured the 100 greatest rock and roll songs of all time are here in this awesome collection! Songs include: Born to Run • Good Vibrations • Hey Jude • Hotel California • Imagine • Light My Fire • Like a Rolling Stone • Respect • and more.
00311110 .... $29.99

River Flows in You and Other Eloquent Songs for Easy Piano Solo

24 piano favorites arranged so that even beginning players can sound great. Includes: All of Me • Bella's Lullaby • Cristofori's Dream • Il Postino (The Postman) • Jessica's Theme (Breaking in the Colt) • The John Dunbar Theme • and more.
00137581 .... $14.99

Disney's My First Song Book

16 favorite songs to sing and play. Every page is beautifully illustrated with full-color art from Disney features. Songs include: Beauty and the Beast • Bibbidi-Bobbidi-Boo • Circle of Life • Cruella De Vil • A Dream Is a Wish Your Heart Makes • Hakuna Matata • Under the Sea • Winnie the Pooh • You've Got a Friend in Me • and more.
00310322 .... $17.99

Top Hits of 2019

20 of the year's best are included in this collection arranged for easy piano with lyrics. Includes: Bad Guy (Billie Eilish) • I Don't Care (Ed Sheeran & Justin Bieber) • ME! (Taylor Swift feat. Brendon Urie) • Old Town Road (Remix) (Lil Nas X feat. Billy Ray Cyrus) • Senorita (Shawn Mendes & Camila Cabello) • Someone You Loved (Lewis Capaldi) • and more.
00302273 .... $16.99

Get complete song lists and more at
www.halleonard.com

0320
239